Live Again Our Mission Past

by
George Kuska, *AIA, California Architect*
Barbara Linse, *Educator and Author*

with
Mary L. Prosser Flaim, *Specialist, Social
Studies Education*

Art Direction/Production . . . . Ken Gillespie
Mission Drawings. . . . . .George Kuska
Activities Drawings . . . . Cynthia D. Clark
Photography . . . . Wayne G. Hahn
Elementary Education Consultant. . . . . Bernice Gilardi
Editor . . . . Anita Shelasky
Manuscript Preparation. . . . . Pamela Williams Watts
Young Authors . . . . James Byrnes
Serri Miller
Typesetting. . . . . Graphic Express

Published by
ARTS' BOOKS
Larkspur, CA

Distributed by
EDUCATIONAL BOOK DISTRIBUTORS
222 Madrone, Larkspur, Ca 94939

Copyright - 1983 / First Printing 1984
Library of Congress No. 83 - 072050

ISBN 0 - 9607458 - 1 - 5

Dedication

This book is dedicated to Gary De Mirjyn, Director Academia Hispaño Americana, San Miguel de Allende, Guanajuato, Mexico.

Gary was born in Redlands, California, and attended the University of Redlands in that city. His major was Latin American studies.

The many Californians who study at his school have a much greater than average understanding of Spanish California, and of the Mission culture which propelled it into existence.

Barbara Linse

p.s. Never serve atole cold!

Acknowledgments

We gratefully acknowledge recipes from *Katherine Williams* who has developed many for her fine Mexican Cooking School at 115 Jamaica Avenue, Tiburon. To *Narsai David,* thanks for your special vegetable pazole. Thanks: *Monsignor Kennedy* of Mission San Rafael and *Brother Timothy* of Mission Santa Barbara for sparkly ideas.

We appreciate the fine assistance of *Susan Vignes,* curriculum coordinator for the Department of Education, the Catholic Archdiocese of San Francisco.

We appreciate the generosity and enthusiasm of those administrators of the Oakland Museum and the California State Parks System *(Sonoma Region Office)* who made our photographs, taken on their premises, possible.

The California State Park System *(Sacramento Region)* provided direction and descriptions for such topics as Indian Games, Bartering, Adobe, Candle and Soap Making. Our California State Park System and the Oakland Museum are top resources for parents, teachers and children.

We thank most heartily: *James B. Alexander and Fred Welcome* for the little bits and pieces of suggestions and for the sad story of *Howard, The Rejected Rancho Chicken.* To *Donald Brenneis,* Professor of Social Anthropology at Pitzer College, and *Dewey Chamber,* Professor of Education at University of Pacific, so many thanks for expertise in their wondrous disciplines.

Our thanks go to Chapman College and Mission San Juan Capistrano for such liberal use of their archeological findings, and to *Kristie Butterwick* for her charming mural at that Mission.

Our grateful thanks to the Miwok Indian Museum, Novato, California for their fine staff members, who shared their books, their crafts and their enthusiasm for the wonderful world of the California Indians before the Mission period.

We appreciate so much the beautiful colored scenic photographs share by *Bob and Margaret Orr.*

A very special thanks is given to the children who are photographed popping from pots, dipping candles, rubbing noses with donkeys, weaving on the big looms and engaging in other activities of that earlier era. *Michelle and Wayne de Fremery, Ross and Hadyn Murray, Amy and Mickey Lippett,* thanks. *Tony and Carrie Watts,* a special thanks to you. You two were shot so often it's great you are still alive!

We thank those talented fourth graders in *Ruthe Lindlum's* class at Dixie School District who illustrated the *Calexto Legend.* Hooray for *Bill Dittman,* owner of the Marin Teacher's Store, who observed that this book is needed in the homes and schools of California. And thanks, *Aunt Margaret!*

Most especially we thank those valiant fourth grade teachers who interrupted their own programs to have special Mission Murals. Story Boards and Dioramas: *Claire Mosconi and Marita Randolph* of Neil Cummins School and *Adrienne Sweeting* of Hidden Valley Schools in Marin County, California. To *Mrs. Meister* of Saint Anselm's School, we thank you for that Saturday morning in June when we photographed your fourth graders' Missions. The real fourth grade teacher of this book is *Mary Beth Forrest* of Hoover School in Palo Alto. For 2 years we visited her classroom frequently as her youngsters shared Indians; Missions and Ranchos, and even let us pan a little gold. All this is a part of California's heritage. *Serri Miller and Larisa Crapo* were both from *Mary Beth's* classroom. We acknowledge and appreciate the help given by each of you.

Table of Contents

Introduction

Live Again Our Mission Past is presented to help each of the
California Missions gain new life.

You as parents, teachers and other participants are encouraged
to use it fully. Become introduced to earlier times through the
Acorn-Nutshell summaries; make copies of the plays for simple
or more complicated enactment, and the Legend of Calexto
for everyone's fun and a clearer understanding of the two
Californias, Baja and Alta, and their similarities and differences.

The beautiful Mission drawings would be very nice in almost
any home or classroom, and the recipes in any kitchen. The
activities are meant to create and permit a clearer understanding
of the life during these times through simulation or participa-
tion. The Haul of Records is for bits and pieces, great and
small. The history-geography gives a sound background of the
time and place.

Some people may read through the book; some may start at the
middle and read their way to either end. Others may go from
the end to the beginning and some may play hopscotch, going
hither and thither.

This is a book with something special for every California
Mission enthusiast. Those among you who teach are invited
to photocopy anything for distribution within your classroom.

We invite you to join us in this adventure. Dip a candle. Have
a fiesta. Visit a Mission. Read a legend. There's lots of fun
waiting for you.

GEORGE KUSKA
BARBARA LINSE

A Child's Story

Living With California Indians
James Byrnes

Indian children worked hard but they had time for fun too. They played games like hockey. The players had curved wooden sticks and a wooden ball. Another game was hoop and pole. The hoop was rolled on the ground and they would try to throw a pole through the hoop. Basketball was played and tug of war. They liked guessing games and a game like "Button, Button" and dice games played with walnut shells. They would bet on these games and sometimes lose their homes and food.

Girls had dolls and cradles and boys had small bows and arrows. They also played a game like hopscotch and hide and seek.

There were lots of children in the village because everyone lived together. Boys and girls could wander from family to family and live with a second set of parents. They could stay with them and sleep with them.

Indian children wore clothes made of hides. In the winter they wore clothes on top of each other for warmth. Women made the clothing.

Children learned by doing. They learned from their parents and hunters. Girls learned to treat leather for clothes and how to take care of babies.

Boys were given tests for bravery.

Indian children had a hard life compared to our life today. When the white men came to the Indian lands they made their life even harder by taking their land and bringing white man's diseases.

Boys and girls learned never to cry out loud. They might give their position away to an enemy or scare animals.

Indian children learned by making mistakes. They were not told that fire burned. They

learned by   burning their fingers.
　　When a boy was ten, he
was expected to hunt
On his first hunt he couldnt
keep any of the food for
himself. He had to share it
with everyone.
　　When a boy was 12, he had
to go to the mountains far away
by himself with no food for
4 days.

I ndians believed everything
had a spirit. Girls did the
same thing.

In an Acorn Shell

The Indians affected by the California Missions were dwellers along the coast and inland to fifty miles or so, from San Diego to Sonoma. Though these people were from twenty-seven separate tribes, they shared a good life with one another. Their land yielded a bounty of good things. They didn't have to travel far for food and shelter. Each tribe spoke a different language. When the Indians lived together in the Missions they were taught Spanish.

These coastal Indians, though living in separate tribes, shared many things Their economy was based on hunting and collecting. They had similar topics for myths, legends, and folktales.

Food was plentiful and included; from the tidelands, shellfish, and surf fish; acorns from six or seven oak species; salmon and trout from the ocean area; buckeyes, pinenuts, lake and river fish, and land mammals from the foothills. The climate was so mild that the land was like an even-changing menu with various nuts and berries and blossoms and fruit ripening at about the same time each year. Acorns, leached and ground provided a real food staple. The land yielded the goods for home dwellings. Thatched tule and willows were used as weather indicated, and as they were available. In

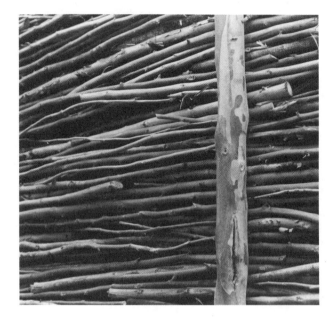

moderate to cold weather tule was used. Shelter from cold and rain was provided by the use of thicker thatch. Bundles of willows or wood were used also.

Baskets and pots were made and used and these generally warm, accepting people had time to decorate them. Mortars and pestles were made and used for grinding acorns. Shoes were made of rush or leather. Fur robes were used in winter, and tule mats were very nice for the floor covering. Babies were diapered in rich, soft moss.

Musical instruments played a real role in the life of the tribes. Pebbles in cocoon rattles, bird bone whistles and elderberry flutes were among the instruments creatively fashioned.

Clam disk beads, *(as shown)*; stone or wood tobacco pipes; a multitude of herbs for medicine; carved arrow heads; soap stone for washing; cooking vessels and bird bone earrings were among the materials used by these Indians.

The Indians played some games that will be listed and described here. The "game time" only constituted a portion of their week's activities. It was to this happy atmosphere that the Spanish came.

Parents, boys and girls, and teachers — write to the State Indian Museum, 111 I Street, Sacramento, California 95814, for more information. (Telephone *(Telephone (916) 445-4204)*

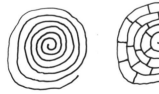

The coastal Indians of California had good lives. The land and climate worked together to provide an abundance of resources — among them, materials for:

California Indian Baskets

California Indian baskets come in a wide variety of sizes, shapes, and patterns. Seventy-eight different plant species have been identified in such baskets. Willows were probably the most frequently used of the plant materials. They were the most acceptable, the strongest, and most resilient. They needed to be peeled and soaked, and were used for warp and weft.

The coil method was commonly used in basket making and a tight weave can be thus obtained.

Take the wet willow or other base or warp materials and wind it into a circle or, yes, a coil.

With even stitches, weave the coiled pieces together. For this, use a tapestry needle and a slender piece of the willow or other native California plant.

As you build the side simply continue adding willow warp and securing it with willow weft or other flexible material until you have the basket you wish.

To make a firmer basket, knot the weft *(weaving fibre between stitches)*.

This is a mere beginning. Books, classes, films, and museums will furnish you with many more ideas on making baskets as the Mission and other California Indians did.

Time Line

	1542	1602	1769
California	The Indians were hunting and gathering food; leaching acorns; making dwellings from wood or tules; and catching fish or jumping into the sweat house.		
Spanish Explorers	Cabrillo explored and died in Alta California	Viscaino traveled up the coast and turned back	First actual settling in California

How Do They Make their Shelter?

They would first gather tule leaves Then they dried them. And then they made a frame out of the willow bark.

Then they stitched the sides of the house. They made the sides out of willow poles.

Then they put up the stitched sides over the frame.

Inside the house, they dug holes in the ground for the beds and a hole in the roof for the smoke to escape.

What are the Women Doing?

The women make baskets.

The women make their own cradles for the babies.

They pick berries for the evening meal.

They cook the evening meal.

They pick weeds and let them dry.

Then they take all the seeds off with a split wooden stick.

Then they weave the dry weeds. They also put red and black in the baskets for looks

The baskets are finished. It took many days until it was done.

The men first walk to the steam room

They start a fire in the fire pit.

They wipe the sweat off them with split deer ribs.

When the men can't stand the heat any longer they jump in the lake, river, pond, etc.

The Legend of Calexto: the Make-Believe Maker of Alta and Baja California

Calexto was the Creator God of the Californias. He was so bold and selfish that the other gods didn't want him around. He was so pleased with his first creation that he didn't want to share it. He shouted to the east that Alta California was an island *(it wasn't!)*, so that he could keep it for himself and his most precious Indians.

He gave them many wonderful things; food and beauty from the sea, streams of fresh water and a nice climate. There were plenty of seeds and berries for the Indians to eat, hills to protect them from the wind, wood and willows to build shelters, and reeds for making baskets tight enough to carry water, and to cook fish and meat. There were round rocks for grinding acorn meal and other things. In fact, he was so good to the Alta California Indians that many of them had beautiful rabbit fur coats and moss with which to diaper their babies.

When he saw how beautiful his Alta California was, he was afraid that newcomers might come from the south and take it from him, so he decided to make Baja California a barrier to keep them out. He would create a land that would tempt people to come but would be difficult and challenging enough so that they would have to work hard to live there and would stay away from his precious Alta California.

When he heard that explorers had discovered the new world of which the Californias were a part, he said, "I must keep the California Island Story alive so that those snoopers won't come and take away this beautiful land." So he shouted it again, "Alta California is an island!" and the wind carried his voice into the right listening ears.

The explorers stayed away from Alta California. Calexto caused trouble in Mexico to keep Cortez busy, and dropped pearls in the bay at La Paz to keep the attention of explorers on Baja California. Cabrillo might have spread the word about Alta California, but while he was still in Baja, Calexto had pushed him into the yerba flecha, a herb that causes temporary blindness, which caused him to fall in San Diego, break his arm, and die of the infection. His log books, recording all he had seen

until his death in Santa Barbara, were sent to the King of Spain.

Later, the travels of Viscaino brought another threat to Calexto's plans. There were now many doubts about the island story, and Calexto didn't want anyone to get close to Alta California. When Viscaino was coming along the coast, Calexto sent a big fog to cover some of the best harbors, so that Viscaino wrote in his log that someone else should look at it again.

When the Jesuit priests decided to bring Catholicism to the Indians of Baja California, Calexto wanted to make sure they wouldn't go farther north.

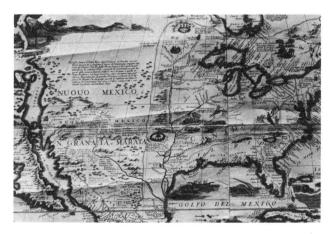

"This is the Mexico you know," Calexto whispered to the wind. "Look what happened to your brothers in Alta California, Cabrillo and Viscaino. One died and the other was fogged out."

The kind Jesuit Fathers heard these whispers as they went about their work in Baja California. It was close to Mexico, and after all, wasn't Alta California possibly an island? Didn't bad things happen to everyone who tried to explore it? "The Indians here need our help," the fathers said. "They can't even get enough food."

The King of Spain got a message or two telling of pools of pearls and mountains of silver in Baja. Do you suppose Calexto sent the words?

The priests wanted to help these poor, hungry Indians get more from the meager land, and Calexto wanted to keep them away from Alta California. He got the Indians and Spaniards to work together building the first chapel of palm thatch, and then, when the heat got to him, Calexto left them working and went to Alta California to enjoy the delicious food and good climate.

Back in Baja California, Calexto decided to reward the hard working people by giving them some good things. He created the wild fig, zalati, which grows in crevices of rock, and the organ cactus, which bears a nectar-like fruit for two full months in the

summer. He added tiny snapdragons, popcorn flowers and lots of palm trees; these had no fruit, but gave promise of better things to come.

So the people worked harder and harder to stay in Baja, where the land was beautiful but rain and food were scarce. Despite the difficulties, the first Mission was built at Loreto, on the coast, with large rocks and mortar. Between 1697 and 1768, twenty Missions were built in Baja California. Calexto's great plans were succeeding.

But perhaps Calexto was becoming too smug and self-satisfied. Certainly he was becoming fat from all the delicious food in Alta California, and sometimes he was too lazy to keep careful watch on what the explorers were doing. He would take long naps after his big meals, and while he was sleeping, Spain was making plans that would ruin Calexto's private paradise forever. The Jesuits left Baja and the Franciscans came for a year. When Portola and Father Serra traveled to San Diego to start the first Mission in Alta California, Calexto sent storms to delay the ships, and tried to stop the land travelers with hunger and disease. By now Calexto's powers, along with his muscles, were getting weak and this time he could not keep the travelers away.

Once the first settlement was begun, there was nothing Calexto could do to keep California to himself. News of the wonderful climate and pleasant land spread to the rest of the world, and Calexto found himself helpless to prevent people from coming in and making California into one of the most important and beautiful states in a new nation.

And what happened to Calexto, who had made the land for himself and then had to watch it taken over by strangers? No one really knows, but some people say that when he saw the first buildings going up at San Diego, he ran down from the hills and jumped into the sea, causing a gigantic splash. And even now, people say, when the great whales travel slowly along the coast of California, Calexto might be out there with them, forever looking back at the beautiful land he created and lost.

In a Nut Shell

THE BAJA CALIFORNIA INTERVAL

The peninsula of Baja California became the focus of Spanish interest. Stories were told of silver mountains and lakes filled with pearls. During the sixteenth century, Cabrillo, Viscaino, and others had explored the hot, dry, and rather barren land. After Cortez spent a year near the present site of La Paz, Spain decided to have Baja settled by missionaries. In 1697, the Jesuits started the first Mission and colonies, which were easily reached from Mexico across the Gulf of California.

Twenty Jesuit Missions were founded, with great difficulty, in the next seventy years. *(See Great Haul of Records)* Rain was so scarce that almost nothing grew, and the Indians were killed in large numbers by the epidemics which were brought by the Spanish and to which the natives had no natural immunity.

The Mission system was an inexpensive way to colonize a land and its peoples. In the Californias, the priests could build with native materials and could use the food of the land to supplement their diet. Practical crafts were taught to the Indians, and goods were produced in Mission workshops that could be used by the settlement or in trade. Many needed supplies were brought to the Baja Missions, principally from the Far East.

Mission locations were selected where water was accessible and where crops and animal fodder could be grown. While the primary goal of missionaries was to Christianize the natives, they also hoped to establish communities where Spaniards could engage in agriculture.

Despite effort and planning, the Missions in Baja California did not prosper. The land, though pleasant in winter, was too rocky, too dry, and too

hot to encourage settlement. In 1768, the Jesuits' twenty Missions were transferred to the Franciscans and Father Junipero Serra came to Baja as their president.

In the following year, the king of Spain and the Viceroy of Mexico, rereading the notes of Cabrillo and Viscaino describing the green grass and golden flowers of Alta California, ordered Serra to leave the Baja Missions and join Governor Portola's expedition to the north and to establish a Mission at San Diego. This was to be the first of many built in Alta California.

Exploring California

A play to be read together by a group of people, probably children.

The play can be divided into the sections of your choice.

Masks and puppets can do the talking.

Costumes and scenery are not necessary, imaginations will do.

Write your own play in your own ways. Feel free to photocopy *(as shown on title page)*.

SCENE I — 1542

Cast — Storytellers *(can have several)*

    Cabrillo

    Sailor

    Indians

Possible props — Pictures of old maps

        Notebook for ship's log

Storyteller 1

The year is 1542. It was thought that California was an island. Spain owned all of Mexico including, of course, Baja California. Juan Rodriguez Cabrillo, a Portugese explorer, was called on by the King of Spain and the Viceroy, Spain's representative of Mexico, to check out this so called island of Alta California.

Storyteller 2 *(reads a poem for this occasion)*

The Viceroy of Mexico
Said, "Up, Cabrillo, and off you go,
You can have ships and men of all sorts.
Please bring us back some good reports
of Indians and silver and gold.
The very thought just makes me feel bold!
Claim all this wealth in the name of Spain's King
And around the world your praise we'll sing!
The year was 1542.
I'm glad they discovered our land, aren't you?"

Storyteller 1 *(continuing)* — He sailed past the west coasts of mainland Mexico and Baja California and eventually landed at the spot where San Diego harbor now lies. Cabrillo and his men were ready for a good rest.

Cabrillo — This is such a beautiful spot. Look at the green grass and golden flowers. *(Looking at the Indians)* Don't you understand? Don't you speak Spanish? We will name this spot for Saint Diadacus and claim it for Spain. San Diego, that's its name. I must get this all down on my maps and in the ship's log *(Cabrillo picks up map and ship's log)*.

Indian: *(to Cabrillo)* — Your clothes are different, aren't they? You don't understand me? You don't talk as we do.

Storyteller 1 — After some days of rest and a pleasant time on shore with the Indians, Cabrillo and his men and his little boats went on up the coast. They saw smoke on the shore! Was something cooking? Was it cold? They called it "The Bay of Smokes."

Storyteller 2 — This could have been Santa Monica or, perhaps, San Pedro. Cabrillo had put into many ports to get food, so his crew got very little scurvy. They had fresh berries to eat. Cabrillo and his men sailed to Santa Barbara's Channel Islands. They always had little gifts for the Indians, like necklaces and other trinkets.

Cabrillo — We'll call these islands the Santa Barbara Islands and the land nearby Santa Barbara. Whoops, I'm falling *(Cabrillo falls on his arm)*.

Sailor — He's broken his arm, I think. *(turning to Cabrillo)* Be careful, sir! *(Cabrillo exits. He reappears with a sling around his arm)*

Storyteller 1 — The men sailed up the coast of California. They passed *(big sigh)* Monterey Bay and San Francisco. . . . .

Storyteller 2 — But they never really saw the harbors. Maybe it was because these harbors were all fogged in. *(to audience)* What do you think? Soon after, Cabrillo got really sick, because his arm became infected and he died.

SCENE II — 1602

Use new storytellers — *(they can be sons and daughters of other storytellers)*.

Cast — Storytellers

     Viceroy

     Viceroy's Aide

     Viscaino

     3 Sailors

     3 Indians

Possible props — An hourglass

              A clock

              A telescope *(use a paper cylinder)*

              3 small ships

              Paper for log keeping

Storyteller 2 — The year is 1602. The new Viceroy of Mexico was pacing back and forth in his office in Mexico.

Viceroy — We have to do something about Alta California. They say it's an island, you know?

Aide — This new Señor of the sea might be of great help. They say that he is brave and true and never gives up, and he's very good at keeping his ship's log — and we do need someone who writes because there aren't a lot of explorers or anyone else who writes these days, or reads either.

Storyteller 2 — In May of Sixteen Hundred and Two,
Not having anything else to do,
Said a later Mexican Viceroy
"Viscaino, you're quite a boy!
You can have three ships, that's quite a few.
An explorer's life is waiting for you.
From San Diego, please go on North,
And see what the harbors and land are worth.
From Acapulco, sail up the shore,
I don't believe it will be a bore!

Storyteller 1 — They sailed off from Acapulco on May 5, 1602.

Storyteller 2 — Sebastian Viscaino, the explorer, had his trusty hour glass *(and a minute minder, too)*, clocks, telescopes, two hundred men, three small ships and lots of paper for log keeping. He was full of courage.

Storyteller 1 — On November 10, 1602, San Diego was spotted. It had a beautiful natural harbor. The sailors and Viscaino went ashore with happy faces and empty tummies.

Sailor 1 — Ahoy, there. We are here!

Storyteller 2 — Of course, it was said in Spanish.

Sailor 2 — I feel so sick, could it be scurvy?

Sailor 3 — The what?

Sailor 1 — Scurvy, scurvy! You often get it on ships.

(Note: Maybe some of you children can look up scurvy and bring the cure back to 1602)

Indian 1 — Have some acorn mush and clear water from the stream.

Sailor 3 — I wonder what they are saying. Oh, look! Food. I'll try anything. Wow! It's so good!

Viscaino *(writing in his log)* — The natives are wearing rabbit fur capes and deer skin wraparounds.

Storyteller 2 — After some days together, they said their goodbyes to the Indians in Spanish.

Sailors *(as they wave goodbye and leave in their canoes)* — Adios, amigos.

Indian 1 — What are they saying?

Indian 2 — They are going.

Indian 3 — Look at their hands going up and down in the air. That must mean "goodbye."

Storyteller 2 — They sailed on and on . . . . . all three ships.

Viscaino *(with a telescope — paper rolls)* — This must be the harbor we read about in Juan Rodriguez Cabrillo's log.

Storyteller 1 — Viscaino wrote about the green grass and golden flowers in his log. He also wrote of stopping at Monterey Harbor which he described as a sheltered bay with a fine port. He told of white oaks, and live oaks, and fresh water and hills. As they sailed north from Monterey, they sailed past San Francisco Bay, for it was covered by a blanket of fog. The party returned to Mexico and turned in the log to the Viceroy who sent it to the King. It stayed with each successive king until 1769, when the then King of Spain re-read the accounts and decided to settle Alta California. The word was out that the Russians were coming into this land, and it certainly had been proven that it was not an island.

Storyteller 2 — Why didn't anyone go back for 167 years after this?
(Children in the classscan respond with these and with their own answers.)
1. I guess the trip was too hard, and the explorers must have said so.
2. They couldn't carry enough fresh water, and ocean water is too salty.
3. They couldn't take very good food on the ship. It was all salted or dried, but never fresh.
4. It would have taken too much room or gotten rotten if they had taken fresh food.
5. The trip was hard because they never knew how hard the winds would blow against them and how long the trip would take.
6. Lots of people got scurvy, and that's no fun.
7. That's because they didn't have any food to eat with enough Vitamin C, as found in lemons, limes, oranges, grapefruit, and a little bit in most every fruit or vegetable, and even in the brown husks of rice.

In an Acorn Shell

THE EARLY EXPLORERS

Christopher Columbus discovered the Americas in 1492; many explorers from Spain followed him. Their navigational equipment was primitive but functional. Their lack of nutritional know-how created a serious health problem on the journeys. The lack of fresh fruits and vegetables for that long voyage caused many sailors to get scurvy.

Magellan's exploration and discovery of the Philippines in 1521 marked the first 25 years of trading from the East to the New World.

By 1542, not only was Mexico well settled by Spain, but Cabrillo, a Portuguese navigator, sailing for Spain, traveled up the California coast, making notes about the land formation, water depth and other pertinent information. San Francisco Bay was probably in a fog blanket as it was not seen. Cabrillo and his men spent some time in San Diego resting and making friends with the Indians. He fell, broke his arm, and died of infection shortly thereafter on one of the Santa Barbara Channel Islands.

Sebastian Viscaino had spent some time exploring the waters and shores around Baja California. In 1602 he went in search of stopover points for the Manila galleons, and was also authorized to look for new places to colonize. He spent some time on the Monterey penisula and wrote a glowing report of it. He also was prevented by the local fog from discovering San Francisco Bay. Alta California was in this way described and claimed for Spain.

SCURVY: A MEDICAL DEFINITION

"Scurvy is a condition due to deficiency of Vitamin C in the diet marked by weakness, anemia, spongy gums, a tendency to mucocutaneous hemorrhages, and a brawny induration of the muscles of the calves and legs. It often affects mariners at sea and those who use salted meats or few vegetables. Using fresh potatoes, scurvy grass and onions as food, and especially drinking lime juice are preventative measures and a curative treatment."

The 1769 Play
The Franciscans Come to Start the Missions

Cast — Storytellers
        Alexis
        King Carlos of Spain
        King's Aide
        Father Junipero Serra
        Jose de Galvez
        Gaspar de Portola
        Sailor
        Captain
        Missionary
        Doctor Pedro Pratt
        Blacksmith
        Father Crespi
        Captain Rivera

Alexis — I am Alexis. I was born in Russia. We have found fine seal furs in Alaska for the hard Russian winters. We moved down here to Alta California. *(speaking to the storyteller)* Did you hear?

Storyteller 1 — Oh yes, and so did the King of Spain.

(office of the King of Spain)

King Carlos — If we are to own the world, we better get busy with Alta (Upper) California. We have certainly had a bad time with Baja (Lower) California. Spanish settlers don't like the desert, so Alta California suits them fine.

Aide — Oh but, your majesty, the Franciscan Brothers are doing their best in Baja California. The Missions that they work in are nice but the weather is so hot; the ground is very hard and rocky; the crops will not grow; and the Indians are not interested in becoming "neophytes." That's what the Franciscan Brothers call their converted Indians.

Storyteller 2 — Yes, that's the story. The reasons California, Baja and Alta, were settled were to Christianize the Indians and to hold the land for Spain from Russia and other European countries.

King Carlos — The Russians are in Alaska, and some are in Alta California already. I say we take all of the Franciscans out of Baja California and

send them to San Diego. *(He turns to his secretary with a long quill pen and commands)* Write to my man in Mexico, Viceroy Jose de Galvez, and tell him to go to Alta California and start building Missions up the coast. They can hold the land for Spain that way and Christianize the Indians all at the same time.

Storyteller 1 — Well, Galvez got the letter. He went to the town of Loreto, the capital of Baja, and told the plan to Gaspar de Portola, the governor, and Father Junipero Serra, the Mission president.

Father Junipero Serra — We can work with the Indians and help them become Christians and farmers and speak and read Spanish. In about ten years we can leave a group of them and they will be good Spanish Catholic farmers.

Storyteller 2 — They both wanted to help people get on their own feet.

Jose De Galvez — Portola shall stay long enough to establish Monterey, but Father Serra will be head of all the missions and stay until they are all built.

King Carlos *(reading from the diaries of Cabrillo and Viscaino)* — These early explorers talk about green grass and yellow flowers in Alta California, and of friendly Indians. I hope we find success.

(Loreto, Baja California)

Father Junipero Serra and Governor of California, Gaspar De Portola *(singing)* —
We'll start some towns in Alta California
To hold the lands and Christianize the folk.
We'll send two ships a-sailing to San Diego.
The rest of us will walk, and that's no joke.

Father Serra — I hold the position
That we should start with a Mission
And build it with materials around.
With these books on architecture
I won't attend a lecture.
We'll make adobe bricks with sand and ground.
(Some straw for sticking but the main ingredients are sand and clay.)

(Mexico)

(Large group of people gathered in front of a ship and sailors ready to go to San Diego on the first ship)

Sailor — Captain, I'm a sailor on this ship, I guess.

Captain — Well, if you're a sailor on this ship you will have twenty-four shipmates who are sailors. This fine vessel is the *San Carlos*, and we're off to start the town and Mission of San Diego.

Missionary *(calling out with dignity)* — Excuse me, excuse me. I'm a missionary. May I get on the ship?

Blacksmith — And I am a blacksmith. May I get on the ship?

Captain *(carrying ship's log book)* — Will you please jot down that the *San Carlos* sailed from Baja California on January 9, 1769?

Sailor — Yes, sir.

Storyteller 1 — Excuse me. There are some things our audience needs to know. The *San Carlos* took one hundred and ten days to get to San Diego, and most of the people were sick with scurvy because they did a foolish thing and took only dried foods to eat. Also, the ship *San Antonio* left a month later and took only fifty-five days at sea. Then the land parties started out . . . Let's watch the land parties get started.

(on the way to California)

Father Crespi — Captain Rivera, do you think that twenty-five soldiers are enough to take along? Remember, we'll be taking cows, some bulls, horses, mules, tools, food and seed on the mules, and lots of Indians.

Captain Rivera — Oh, Father Crespi, that will be plenty, but I am really counting on you to keep the official diary. I hear you're the best.

Portola — We'll be leaving in a few days. I'll be with Father Serra and Sergeant Ortega. We'll have animals and soldiers and Indians. Be sure, all of you, to find nice grassy places for camping with fresh water. You'll need grass for the animals, you know, and we will carry some water in leather containers. We will also take the architecture books.

Father Serra *(writing in his journal)* — I had a very bad sore on my leg. The head boy of the mules put some wild herbs on it. My sore is getting a lot better now. There are roses everywhere, and I have been eating berries and even grapes in the canyons. It is so beautiful here.

Doctor Pratt — I am Pedro Pratt and I shave Father Serra daily.

Father Serra — This does look like Cabrillo and Viscaino's description of San Diego. Where are the ships?

Storyteller 2 — We are out to finish the play, six months after starting, all four groups are here together in San Diego.

(San Diego)

Father Serra *(hanging a bell on a tree)* — San Diego. We have made it.

Storyteller 1 — The next three Mission sites were selected because of their harbors, fresh water source and position against the mountains. The remaining seventeen Missions in the chain were founded so that they would be only a day apart by horse or on foot.

Note: The days of departure to San Diego:
   January 7, 1769 — the *San Carlos* sailed and the trip took about one hundred and ten days.
   Early February 1769 — the *San Antonio* departed and arrived in San Diego seventy days later.

   Father Crespi, the good diary keeper, and Captain Rivera's land group left on **Good Friday 1769**. They had one hundred and eighty mules and five-hundred domestic animals and many Indians who died or left the group on the way north. They arrived two months later.

   Captain Portola and Father Serra left in **mid-May 1769** and arrived on **July 1**.

EPILOGUE TO THE PLAY

A group of padres and Indians were sitting around a fire at Mission San Carlos in Carmel *(This could be dramatized as Father Serra tells the story, or it could be read in parts.)*

Father Serra — Did you hear about Portola finding Monterey? *(everyone shakes head "no.")* — He was told by the king to find Monterey Bay. You see, Viscaino had written all about this beautiful spot. Well, Portola started off with a small group of men with all of Senor Viscaino's records and went searching for Monterey. They got here but they didn't recognize the shore and another nearby. He felt so bad that he didn't find Monterey Bay *(even though they had)* that he went back to San Diego.

Another Priest — Tell the part about the mules.

Father Serra — Do I have to? Well, all right. The men were so sad and hungry and sick on the way home that they ate their mules to stay alive. I know that to be true. They all smelled like mules — through this very nose *(points to nose)*. When Governor Portola took another land group back to the site of the cross he followed on the *San Antonio*. The cross was right by the harbor all decorated by the Indians with meat, shellfish, feathers and arrows stuck in the earth and with a string of sardines. On June 3, 1770, bells were hung. All of the people came in their very best clothes and the Mission was blessed. We all began to build the Mission and the presidio of Carmel and Monterey right here. I'll never forget the big cannon roll that was like thunder that came right after the dedication on this very spot.

Mission Plans in Alta California

The Viceroy of Mexico told Father Serra: *"You will be head of a new Mission system — at each there will be a church, workshops, small houses, crops, and classes in Spanish and religion."* Crops will be planted; sheep and cattle raised; weaving and basketry, ceramics made for own use; tallow rendering and skin drying which will be used for trade; a chapel for worship; and the buildings and occupants will all be part of the Mission. As soon as the Mission was functioning, the priests would leave and start another Mission, after 10 years.

This ideal included:
- having all the buildings complete and well-equipped kitchens with enough wood stoves and ovens;
- food for preparation, all raised at the Mission;
- Mission craft rooms for self-sufficiency;
- big looms for weaving, and spinning wheels, brought from Boston, for rugs, blankets, and clothing;
- clay for making pots, although most of the pots, dishes and utensils were brought from Mexico and were used for cooking and serving.
- basketry making for gathering, carrying, and storing all sorts of foods;
- adobe making, for new bricks and for building and replacing old bricks.

Sleeping quarters were to have been finished and furnished. Some were not, even when secularization took place. Classrooms were built for teaching religion, and speaking and reading Spanish. Farming skills were to have been mastered, as well as the techniques of candle dipping, tallow rendering and high drying. The chapel was to have been complete as religion was an intrinsic part of each day. The 10 year plan didn't work. Why? The Indians came from the stone age and had so much to learn. For example, it was difficult to teach them to read because of the tremendous intervention of epidemics, earthquakes, Indian raids, and pirateering, all of which was unforeseen. Priests, Indians, and townspeople worked together from the Mission's beginning to the time of secularization.

Education — The Indians were taught Spanish. This was the most practical language to use because of the number of Indian dialects. Certainly the Spanish had to learn some Indian dialects. They had problems to solve and probably all learned together. It was not possible to teach all of the Indians to read, however, because they were so busy.

Here are some thoughts about the basic needs of the Spanish and Indians:
- where are the Indians, in a land that had been theirs?
  They had lived here for centuries.
- how did the Spanish and Mexican and Indian people get along?
- what was the *climate* like for the Spanish settlers?
  The climate of California is like that of Spain. Both areas have Mediterranean climates.
- what changes in *culture* had to be made for both groups?
  As you look through the *food* recipes see who had to make changes.
- what changes took place in *clothing?*
  The Indians expanded their wardrobe with sheep and wool.
  What else might have happened?
- what type of *shelters* were available?
  Spanish started with Indian type and changed to adobe and tiles.

Safety — Had there been earthquakes all through the centuries? It's not healthy for anyone to be in an adobe brick Mission in an earthquake.

Epidemics: The Spanish colonizers unknowingly brought highly contagious diseases to the Indians. The Europeans and Mexicans had built up immunity by contact to such maladies as smallpox and measles. The Indians, on the other hand, had no previous contact with such sicknesses; had no immunity and, consequently, were killed in vast numbers on their initial contact with the diseases.

In an Acorn Shell

MISSIONING IN ALTA CALIFORNIA

The orders arrived from Spain. Father Serra was to take people and supplies from Baja to Alta California to found Mission San Diego de Alcala. Three ships and two land parties set forth on journeys of from three to seven months. Those on the walking trip took with them most of the Mission livestock, including horses, cows, chickens, and sheep. Soldiers and townspeople from Baja came along to found a city and presidio in San Diego. Hunger, scurvy and exhaustion made the trip difficult and caused some deaths along the way.

Two ships, *San Antonio* and *San Carlos,* arrived safely, but a third vessel, *San Jose,* sank with its cargo of food and supplies needed at the Mission. The cargo included 10,000 pounds of dried meat, 1,250 pounds of dried figs, as well as large quantities of beans, raisins, dried fish, wine, and brandy. The ship also carried church vestments for the priests, a big church bell and a variety of bargaining trinkets for the Indians.

Of the original company of soldiers, citizens and priests *(about 110)* only half actually arrived at San Diego. Desertion as well as death had depleted their numbers. The last of the four groups arrived in San Diego on July 1, 1769.

Although the Indians of this region were well-fed and more peaceful than the Indians of Baja California, some were suspicious of the newcomers and protective barriers had to be built around the first Mission.

The original plans of the missionaries were to build and occupy the Missions, teach the Indians to be independent, and then, in ten years, leave. However, they were not able to follow this time schedule.

The moderate climate and abundant rains of California gave the new settlers much hope for their plans. Crops and animals prospered, and new Missions could be built on locations selected for their proximity to fields for crops and grazing, wood for fires, and fresh water.

From 1769 to 1824, the chain of Missions grew. The key Missions were those at San Diego, Monterey, and San Francisco. These three had natural harbors and were given presidios, or formal military installations. After these Missions were located, the others were spaced at intervals of about a day's travel on foot, mule, or horseback. As each settlement was planned, the priests, towns-people and the Indians who would be the Neophytes *(Catholic converts)*, and soldiers would settle in temporary housing of tules or wood and together would decide upon the best location for the Mission.

The Spanish government supplied from $250 to $450 worth of materials yearly, and the Church's Pious Fund sent a starter sum of $1000 for each Mission's purchase of bells, church vestments, tools and seeds. Missions already established nearby would send animals for use and breeding stock, seeds and cuttings for planting, and any other items that could be helpful.

This is the floor plan of a finished Mission, generally made of adobe:

Adobe bricks were made of adobe clay, straw, sand, and water. Straw was often added to hold the mixture together. The mixture was put into wooden molds and sun-dried. These were laid together, end to end and side to side.

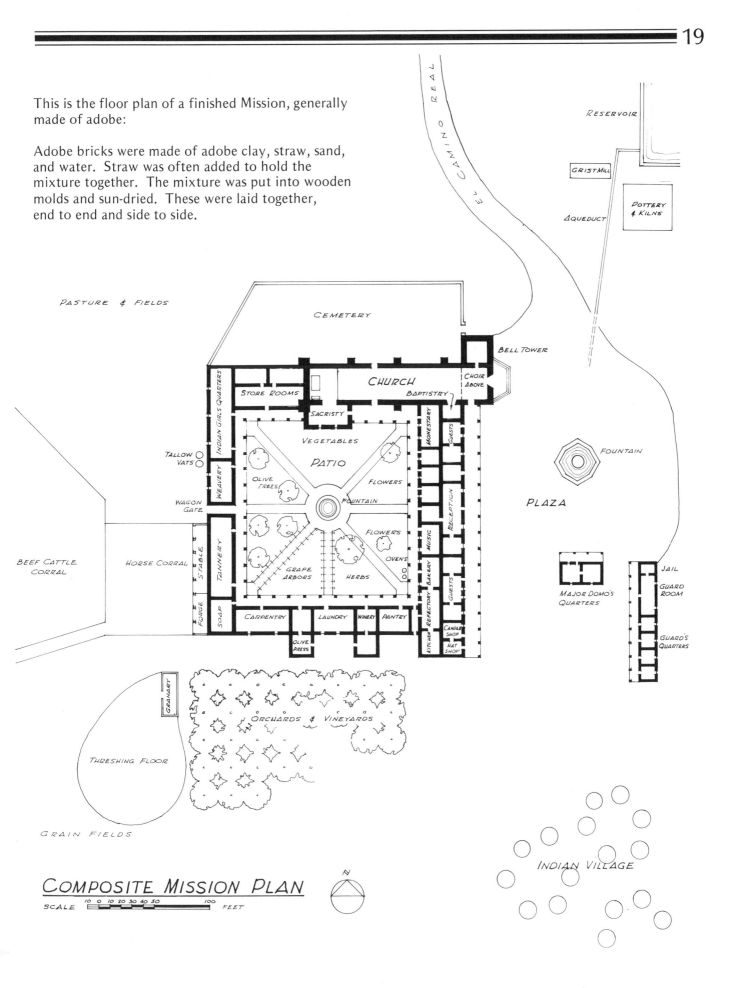

COMPOSITE MISSION PLAN

SCALE 10 0 10 20 30 40 50   100   FEET

A day at the Mission started with bell ringing and prayer, Mass and breakfast. Families would send a big bowl to the Mission kitchen for acorn mush or rice and acornmeal atole. Dinner in the early afternoon might have featured pazole, with or without meat, and supper might be as simple as chocolate and tortillas.

Mission Schools were started to teach the Neophytes the Spanish language. Women were taught practical crafts, spinning, weaving, basket making and kitchen skills. The boys and men spent their days farming, and learning to brand cattle, make olive oil, slaughter and butcher beef, rend tallow, cure hides, dip candles and make soap. These activities were useful to Mission life and reflected the way of life of the larger California community. Religion and Spanish were taught to everyone.

The planned orderly process of Mission building was sometimes affected by natural disasters. Epidemics of common European diseases, such as smallpox and measles, could wipe out half the Indian population of a Mission. California's earthquakes also caused some Missions severe damage, while a few had no quakes at all.

Pagan Indians from the Sierras or desert areas occasionally attacked the settlements. Also, in 1818, the pirate, Hippolyte de Bouchard, raided two Missions and caused alarms at several others.

Trading was an important part of Mission economy. Ships on the long seven-month trip between the United States and Manila used California as a rest stop at first, but later the new colonies could barter their goods for needed items. The Missions' hides, tallow, wine, brandy, and grain were exchanged for tools, furniture, glass, nails, musical instruments, Mexican pottery and cooking vessels, spices and silks from China, Mexican chocolate and Spanish lace.

Vineyards, wineries, olive and citrus groves, cattle and sheep ranches were among the enterprises started by Mission priests in Alta California.

A Child's Story

The Fathers who founded the Missions encouraged Mexican and Spanish citizens with some soldiers to come and establish Ranchos and towns.

The Journal of One Rancher

My name is Pajaro. I own a rancho near the coast of Alta, California. I am married and live with my wife and children on the edge of my land. I acquired it by measuring it with ropes held by my vaqueros. I then made a map of it and took the map to Monterey. (To be granted this land, I must be a Mexican citizen and a Catholic.) A government official will come back to the rancho with me. In the presence of him and the family from the neighboring rancho, I break branches off of trees, pull up grass, and scatter handfuls of earth. This makes the land legally mine.

Our home is well furnished. In our guest room, we have our finest silk pillow-cases, silk sheets, and curtains. We also leave a bowl of money. The guests may take as much as they need, for it is never counted.

We live in the 1800's and our house is built on a square floor plan.

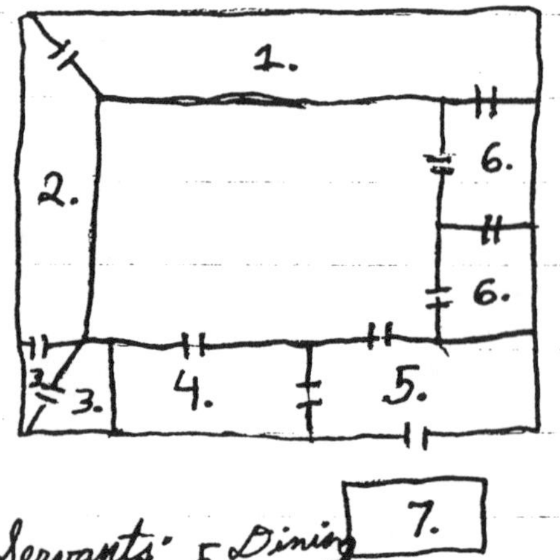

We have thirty Indian servants in all. Ten cook and serve, five do our sewing, six do our washing. Seven are vaqueros and the other two are personal servants.

1. Servants' rooms
2. Living room
3. Storage rooms
4. Guest room
5. Dining room
6. Bedrooms
7. Kitchen
=. Doors

My wife has much work to do. She supervises the servants who do the household work, but her main job is teaching our little girls to sew, make lace, embroider, and play instruments such as the guitar, violin, and flute.

I do very different work, however. I am called el patron. I tell my mayordomo (or foreman) what I want done. I also teach servants to plant trees and crops brought from Spain. We plant wheat, barley, corn, red beans, garbanzos, grapes, onions and garlic. Of trees, we plant olive, peach, apple, pear, and pomegranate. We grow these from cuttings that the Fathers at the Missions give us.

Rodeos

We have rodeos in the springtime, for that is when the calves are still following their mothers. Because of this, generally there is no dispute over which brand the calf will wear. The branding is done by a pair of men. One man will heat his iron in a small, hot fire made of brush while the other catches a calf. The calf is then tied and branded on the flank.

We kill many cattle for their hides. Some of the Indians punch holes in the corners of the hides and set them out in the sun. After the hides are dry, we tan them. Putting a hide into the vat, we sprinkle ground oak bark on it, lay another hide on that one, treat it, etc. Then we soak them in water. Yankee ships come to trade with us, and buy our hides as they did with the Mission Fathers. We bring the hides to the seashore in carratas, a type of ox-drawn cart.

Loss of Rancho

I have decided to sell my rancho, for many of my friends are moving back home. I am selling it legally to a Yankee trader who bought and bartered for our hides. Our family will pack up and leave on May 16, 1842. I am reluctant to leave this rich land.

Postscript on the Rancho Period:

Some Californios *(as the first secular citizens were called)* were fairly poor when they received their ranchos and obtained the land from Spain. Often these rancheros had trouble running their big operation. They had servants, land, and animals. They also had to provide for guests and were expected to be cultured, refined and educated.

As the desire and competition for land increased, many Californios saw that they could make some money by selling their land to "yankees" from the eastern United States. It was common for a family to do this. Many did and returned to a more familiar life in Mexico.

In an Acorn Shell

SECULARIZATION

After Mexico gained independence from Spain in 1810, financial support for the colonists dwindled and the Missions had to become self-supporting. The new Mexican government was not much interested in the Missions, and California's status as a Mexican colony was being threatened by the westward expansion of the United States.

Finally, in 1833, the secularization order was given. As originally planned by the Spanish system, the Missions were to be released and the churches themselves to go from the control of the missionary order to that of the parish priests. Other buildings were to become public property for the new

pueblo, or town, and the land was turned over to the Indian families. Although this system had worked well in other Spanish colonies, it was a disaster in California; the Indians could not manage their new property and were easily deprived of their rights by land speculators. The buildings were sold or simply occupied and property often allowed to deteriorate and disappear. The Missions themselves were nearly forgotten as the entire system was destroyed.

Secularization failed, it would appear, partly because of everyone's land greed. With priests, Indians, and other Mission participants gone, the church lands were frequently taken by the first persons on the spot.

WHAT THE MISSIONS OVERCAME — HARD TIMES CHART

Mission	Earthquake	Indian Raids	Bouchard The Pirate	Indian Epidemics	Secularization	Sold	Returned to Church
San Diego de Alcalá	1803	1775			1834	1846	1862
San Carlos Borromeo de Carmelo			1818		1834		
San Antonio de Padua							1862
San Gabriel Arcángel	1812	1834				1846	1859
San Luis Obispo de Tolosa	1830	1776	1818		1835	1845	1859
San Juan de Capistrano	1812		1818	1801		1845	
San Francisco de Asís				1838	1834		1857
Santa Clara de Asís	1812,1818			Plague Mice	1836		
San Buenaventura	1812		1818		1836	1846	1862
Santa Bárbara	1800,1812	1824			1834	1846	1865
La Purísima Concepcion	1812	1824		1844	1834	1845	
Santa Cruz	1857		1818		1834		
Nuestra Señora de La Soledad				1802	1835	1846	1859
San José		1817,1826, 1829			1834	1846	1865
San Juan Bautista					1835		
San Miguel Arcángel						1846	1859
San Fernando Rey de España	1812				1834		1861
San Luis Rey de Francia					1834	1846	1865
Santa Inés	1812	1824			1834	1846	1862
San Rafael Arcángel		1832			1834	1846	1855
San Francisco Solano		1826			1834	1880	

WHAT HAPPENED TO THE INDIANS?

Here are some answers, you readers, keep looking for more.

1. **Disease: the largest killer**
   The Indians had no natural immunity to such epidemics as malaria, small pox, and measles.

2. **There was almost no medical help for anyone in the Missions**

3. **Culture shock:**
   The Indians were forced to adapt to Mission life and it was a very different life than had been theirs. Of necessity, the Missions were agriculturally self-sufficient, long hours were put in, with few mintues for rest.

The first generation Mission Indians had had great variety in their lives in their tribes and villages. These early Indians felt a loss of freedom and self-expression at the Missions.

There apparently were few children born to Mission Indian couples. The tremendous strain of adjusting to a completely new way of life. According to Heizer and Elsasser, infant mortality was very high.

At the end of the Mission period, from 1769 to 1834, it has been reported that there were one half as many Indians in this Mission area as there had been in the beginning.

After Mexican Independence came the Rancho period. During this time the Indians were generally used as slaves or peons. They cleaned the houses and farmed the land and worked the cattle of their wealthy patrons.

The Indians living away from the Mission areas were pretty much left alone.

Though the Gold Rush didn't take place in Mission locations, its effect on other Indian tribes was significant. Miners and settlers swarmed into the interior valley and the gold bearing regions of the Sierra. The Indians native to those areas had known of the abundance of gold, but not until the white man came to claim it did the gold cause trouble. The miners poured in, and there was competition for food; many massacres of the Indians ensued.

By 1910, the Indian population of California fell to about 20,000 people.

We see in this Mission story, one culture imposing itself upon another. The Spanish appeared to feel that they could give the Indians a better life through the Mission system. Did they?

Were the Indians safer in adobe brick buildings in earthquakes; healthier around the white man's diseases? Were they more contented eating the white man's food? Did it comfort them to serve a god who was strange to them?

Where have all the Indians gone? With the children around you explore these questions and think of many more. If we cannot grow from the examination of those who lived before us, they have almost lived in vain.

THE ROLE OF WOMEN

The role of women in California's early Spanish history cannot be fully dealt with here. At present, there are very few records describing the work and contributions of women in Spanish California. This does not mean that women played no part in the carving of the early history of the State. The work of historians continues; lost treasure troves of documents are being found every year, but the available records appear to be incomplete.

The usual roles of Indian men and women are given in the introduction without, as Margaret Mead emphasizes, any judgment as to the value of the roles. Let's never make any judgments with ourselves and the children of our circle that would demean a person or group for the task rendered.

In most of the Indian tribes of coastal and near coastal California it would appear that, generally, the women prepared the food, did most of the parenting (though most of the Indian group members were innovative and supportive in this area), and created most of the beautiful baskets.

Close your eyes and take every building and non-Indian out of California and you are ready to envision the beautiful, tranquil land of these Indians and to start the exploration and colonization story.

REJUVENATION

During the years, an occasional photographer or painter would share a visual fascination for the Missions through pictures taken, drawn or painted. Some of these pictures grace the walls of special Missions today.

Through the early 20th century, as the automobile took us more places and as El Camino Real developed, Mission restoration began. Sir Harry Downy, called the Mission restoration architect, used time and money to generate much enthusiasm for this exciting project.

At this writing all of the Missions have gone through, or are going through, restoration and are living again.

Most Missions are living, perhaps, most vitally as parish churches. Two are California State Parks. In this restored, "live again" life, tourism is stimulated, weddings are celebrated, funerals are given, and baptisms give new life.

Mission authenticity is looked for and respected!

A LIVING MISSION

The Palo Mission — address to Mission San Luis.

First founding: 1816. An asistencia or helping Mission, Palo is also an inland Mission. In 1818, the chapel of San Antonio was enlarged and completed. Two large granaries were built, as were dormitories for boys and men and for girls and women. These were fashioned from adobe and had red tile roofs.

Palo Mission Indians are Shoshoneans, called Luisenis since early Mission days. The Mission was abandoned with the others, but in May 1902 it was bought by the Landmark Society.

In 1956, a complete reconstruction was promised which was to include the founding of a school. There were problems and roadblocks, but today Palo Mission is restored and has a successful school, and a church membership of Indians that is unique in the present California Mission System. Palo Mission is alive, well, and an example of "living again."

Visualizing Historical Events

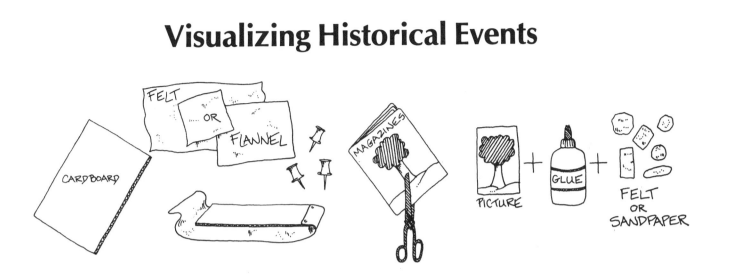

FLANNEL BOARDS

Cover a board or large sheet of cardboard with felt, flannel, or sandpaper. Cut out pictures from paper or magazines, for Mission days story telling. Glue felt, sandpaper or flannel on the back of the pictures. Use these for storytelling by putting them on and off and here and there.

Materials — Scissors
— Paper
— Magazine pictures
— Colored paper
— Big board - felt, flannel or sandpaper
— Glue

MISSION FROM BAKER'S CLAY

Mix; add color; and wrap to insure moistness. You can roll the walls and add texture, as shown. Put these little missions together by wedging or pressing corners together. Bake at 325° for 2 hours. You may save some assembly work until the end.

Materials — Salt, flour, water
— Tempera paint
— Plastic wrap
— Model materials

DIORAMAS

Make a real scene depicting Indian Mission or
rancho days in 3-D. Put paper tabs on paper
figures to make them stand. Sponges make good
bushes and bushy trees. Paint them with tempera.

Materials

— Shoe boxes — Colored paper
— Scissors — Sponges - twigs - etc.
— Paste or glue — Magazine pictures

NEWSPAPER

Make a newspaper; use various parts of the paper to shed light on the life of a particular event, such as earthquake news, recipes, the latest fashions, and growing things.

How to Do It

Really study the newspaper and its various parts. Determine who will do what, such as feature writer, travel, economics, or bartering. You may want to bill jobs, such as editor-in-chief, news editor, weather forecaster, etc. Advertise for adobe makers, muleteers, and gardeners.

Application

This will give participants a chance to really look over various mission times and rewrite special events and daily life that took place during this time.

Materials — Will depend on your way with the newspaper

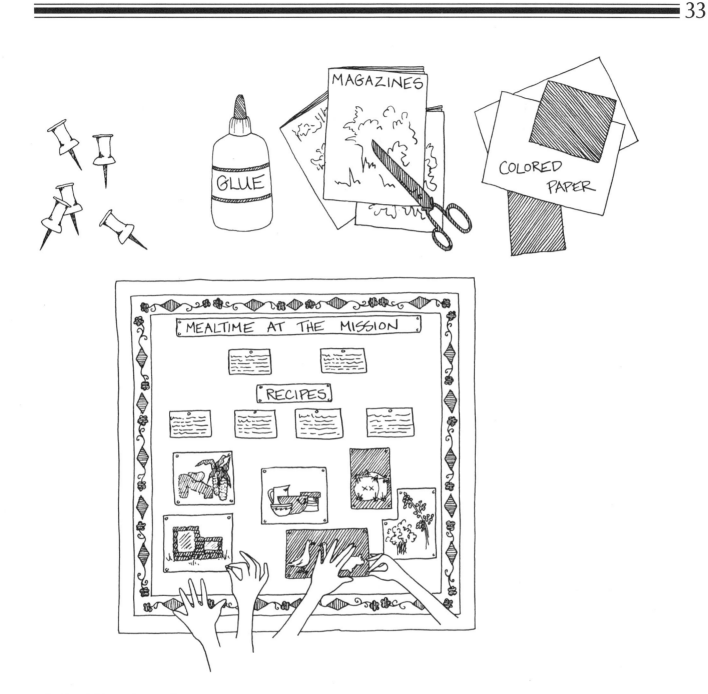

BULLETIN BOARDS

Select your theme and use both written and pictured concepts to bring it to life. Notice the border of Mission designs.

Materials — Display materials
         — Scissors
         — Glue
         — Colored paper for background
         — Push pins

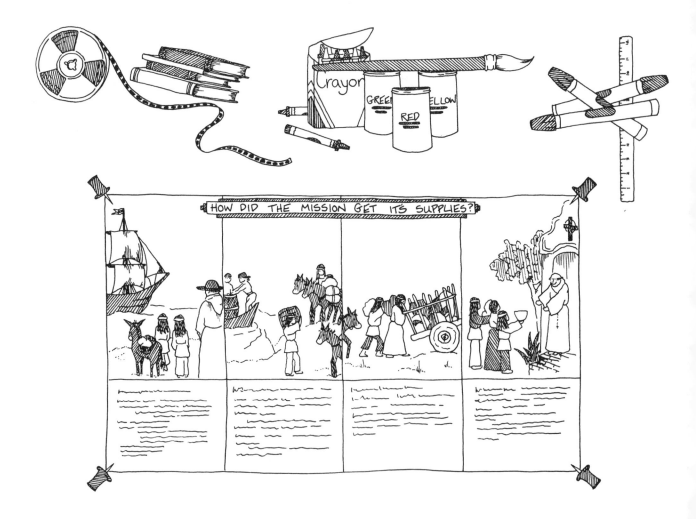

HOW DID THE MISSION GET ITS SUPPLIES?

STORY BOARDS

Background: traditionally, motion pictures are started with storyboards — a sequence of pictures and the accompanying script, as shown.

Be sure to explore the topic, such as Mission supplies, so the artist-writer can approach the task with confidence. Paints, crayons, and felt pens are the best tools. Any phase of California history is suitable for storyboards.

Materials — Paper, pencils or pens
— Crayons, paint or felt pen markers

MISSION MOBILES

Natural materials found in California or Mission themes, such as animals cut from cardboard and painted are fine. Magazine pictures may be glued onto cardboard and cut, too. Notice the coat hanger and umbrella mobiles?

Materials — Wire hangers or umbrella
— Magazine pictures mounted on cardboard
— Nature materials
— Thread
— Scissors

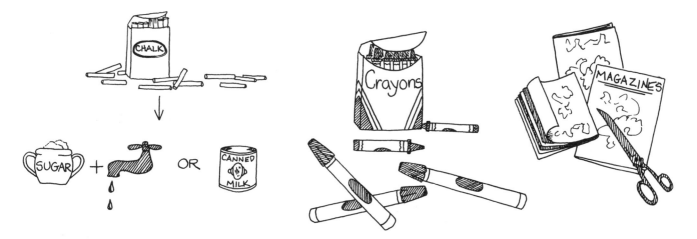

MURALS

1. Select a theme
2. Select a group or do the mural yourselves.
3. List contents of the mural. Let it make a
   statement or tell a story.
4. Sketch it on butcher, shelf or manila paper in
   white chalk.

Use paint, chalk *(use dry chalk, wet chalk, wet and
sugared chalk, or chalk dipped in canned milk),*
crayons, cut paper or magazine pictures for telling
the story. These can be telling a single event or
a series, as shown.

Materials — Paper
— Chalk
— Crayons
— Magazine
— Colored paper
— Scissors
— Glue

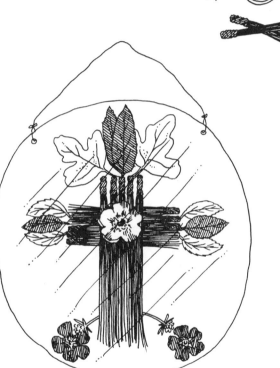

NATURE SHEETS: from pretty outdoor things and waxed paper. You can really see the light.

How to Do It

Put one sheet of waxed paper on a newspaper; lay leaves, berry skins, pine needles, etc. Cover with the wax paper and iron.

Application

On an "Indian and Mission" walk pick up all sorts of light things that the Indians and Mission folks might have loved.

Materials — Nature pieces
           — Waxed paper
           — Iron

A CALIFORNIA RUB DOWN

Using white, manila or typing paper with crayons rubbed over such surfaces as those shown. If these are nicely cut and matted they will make good looking wall pieces.

Materials — Paper
— Crayons
— Textured surface

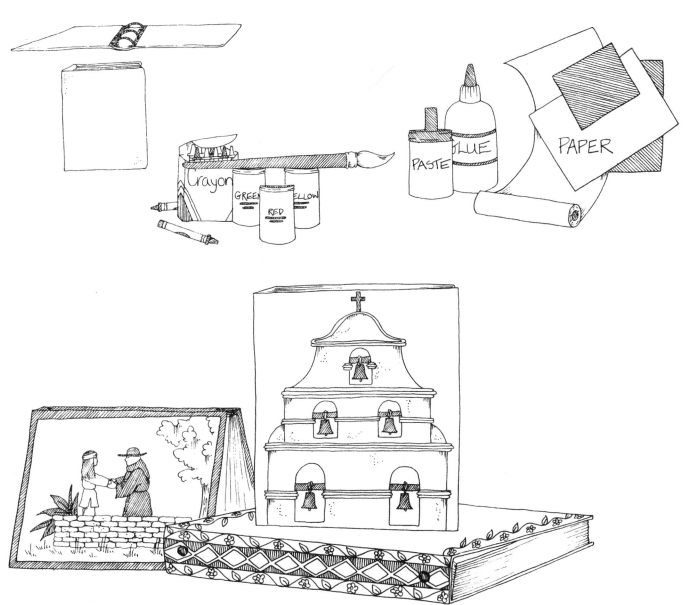

NOTEBOOK COVERS

Use a binder or make a paper or cardboard folder
for holding Mission papers and pictures. Center on
a theme and decorate for open house at school or
happy saving at home. Crayons, paints or cut
paper are fine for decorating.

Materials — Notebooks
 — Colored paper
 — Paint
 — Crayons
 — Paste
 — Scissors

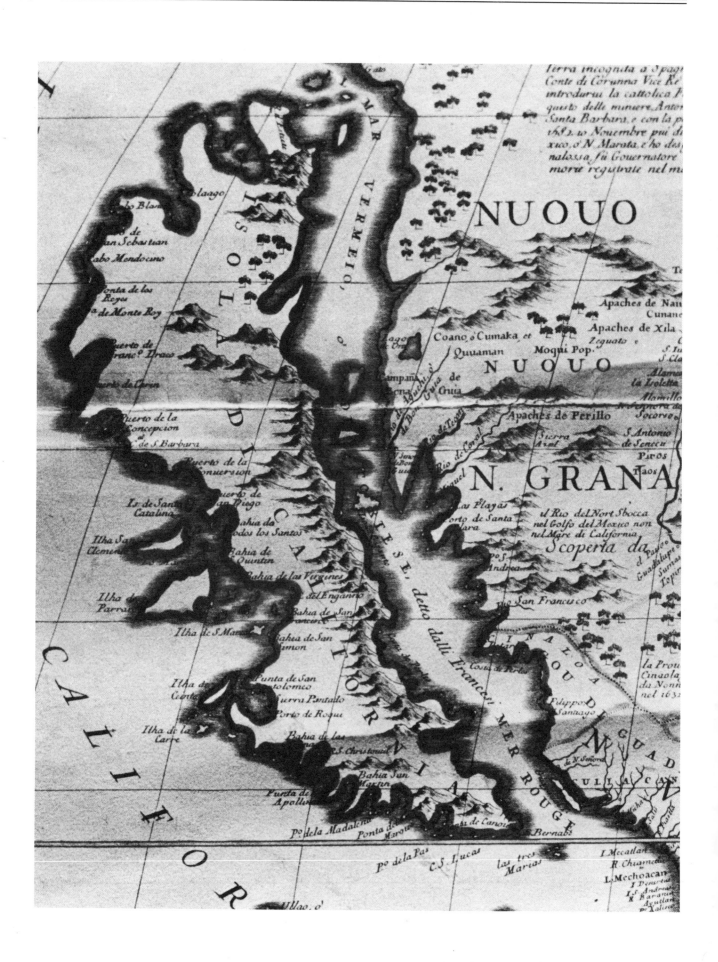

Historical Settlement and Its Relationship to Physical Geography of California's Mission Period

by Mary L. Prosser Flaim

Hispanic culture has made a number of lasting impressions on the southwestern part of the United States, in particular California. The El Camino Real, use of irrigation, introduction of grapes and wine-making, mission architecture, and even the name of the state are but a few of the contributions which may be directly attributed to the Spanish. The Spaniards were drawn to California for several reasons. There was a need to locate and colonize harbor sites for ships sailing the Pacific coastline. In addition, the threat of foreign pirates sailing the same waters accentuated the need for protective settlements. The clergy recognized the desire to convert the native Indians from paganism to Christianity. Thus a frontier was opened by the cooperative efforts of clergy and military.

The similarities of climate and landforms between the coastal mountains of California and the Spanish part of the Iberian Peninsula enabled the Mission founders to recognize and realize the natural potentials of the region. The immigrants and the imported plants and animals easily adapted to Alta California's climate; therefore, the padres were able to actualize their survival needs without a long waiting period of trial and error acclimatation. Site selection of the Missions was crucial, for location contributed greatly to the success or failure of each project. When choosing a site, three factors of consideration were arable soils, convenient water supplies, and a large local Indian population. The landforms and climate of the locale determined, to a large extent, if an area did or did not provide these factors. The Baja peninsula is a harsh, dry region. The priests struggled in the arid rocky soils of Baja for over 100 years to develop an agriculturally based economy on which to subsist as they worked to convert the peninsular tribes.

When Father Serra and his supporters began the missioning period of Alta California in 1769, they focused on the three factors of site determination stated above. The land and climate were more varied, more pleasant, and the soils more fertile than in Baja. The Missions in Alta California flourished under the guidance and skills of the Franciscans.

To better understand the importance of the site requirements, it is necessary to first turn back in time prior to 1769 and examine the historical settlement of California's past. Following the review of settlement during the missioning period, a discussion of landforms and climate of California is presented. Neither section is purported to be a complete synthesis of information available on California's history or physical geography. For these readers who desire further information on these topics, a suggested readings list of geographic texts is included. Teachers are encouraged to use the maps, not only for classroom study of California, but for other regional examinations too. Some of these are quite brief and were drawn as such. The author intends for these maps to be utilized as base materials for the children and hopes instructors find them helpful for many purposes.

Historical Settlement of California During the Missioning Period

Spain was united into one nation in 1469 with the marriage of King Ferdinand and Queen Isabella. The land was financially drained after years of internal political and military strife and was recovering slowly. With crusading spirits and a need to replenish the treasury, these two monarchs supported explorations into uncharted seas. Expeditions had two purposes: to search for profitable lands and to search for potential sites for colonization to protect profits from pirates.

Business agreements were made with explorers so that new lands and treasures could be claimed for the Spanish crown. Spain's closest competitor in this race was Portugal; but the rulers of other nations, including England, Holland and Russia, also supported or permitted exploration and settlement. Often the same lands were claimed by several nations. Spanish settlements were planted by armies or priests; but actual colonization was necessary to prevent other countries from permanently settling or claiming the same area.

Valuables discovered, as well as the land, became

the property of the Motherland. The members of the expeditions were awarded a portion of the wealth by various means. Colonies were established to restrain the natives and serve as depositories of goods awaiting shipment to Spain. The settlements were in fact developed by cooperative efforts between the clergy and the military. Where the native populations were suspicious or hostile, the military advanced first, as the conquistadores led by Cortes did in Mexico; but if the natives were known to be peaceful and receptive to the Spanish, the clergy went first, accompanied by a small military escort. This was the method of California's settlement.

The shipping of pearls, spices, silks, china, gold and other items required a long and dangerous journey across the Pacific and Atlantic Oceans. After collecting the precious cargos from colonies scattered through the Far East, slow and cumbersome Manila galleons would set sail for Mexico enroute home to Spain. Just crossing the Pacific took seven months. The treasure ships sailed across the Pacific Ocean aided by the North Pacific Current, a kind of giant river flowing in a clockwise direction in the northern part of that sea. Some ships stopped for fresh water, food and ship repairs after reaching the western coast of North America. Most, however, chose to continue the journey to Mexico. The sailors feared attack by hostile tribes or pirates *(such as the Englishman Sir Francis Drake).* Many sailors were dying due to the ravages of scurvy, so weak that they were unable to drop anchors and sails to rest. There was a definite need to colonize the coastline of Alta California as aid stations for the Manila galleons; but that plan was shelved for several centuries as Spain focused intensely upon the Aztecs of Mexico and the Incas of Peru. The few encounters with the coastal California tribes did not promise instant rewards, for those Indians were not highly civilized and did not show the Spanish great caches of gold, silver or other minerals to whet the Spanish appetites of wealth.

In 1542, Cabrillo sailed north along the western Baja and Alta California coasts from Mexico. He was followed sixty years later by Viscaino in 1602. Both expeditions were seeking a shorter route to the Orient for the Manila galleons and looking for natural harbors and potential sites for settlements. Neither party explored inland beyond the coastal bluffs to find the fertile valleys known today; nor did they see evidence of California's mineral wealth. In addition, neither party noted San Francisco Bay which was probably fogbound, thus passing by this protected body of water, potential aide station site, and the convenient route to the interior lands. Cabrillo discovered and mapped San Diego harbor, the only natural deep water port in southern California. Viscaino discovered Monterey Bay and described it as a fine sheltered harbor; however his enthusiastic writing about the bay was misleading to future expeditions. Persons who have visited that area know it to be a wide open arc of coast-line and not, as Viscaino wrote, "the best port that could be described. . .very secure against all winds." Although Viscaino had been wrong in his assessment of Monterey Bay, his voyages up and down the Baja and Alta California coasts from 1596-1622 provided some of the best maps for the next 200 years.

Valid and false information was accumulated by sailors, missionaries and conquistadores as future expeditions were launched. A major myth circulating during the 16th and 17th centuries was that all of California was an island. This probably resulted from two sources. The first was a romantic novel published about 1500. **Las Sergan de Esplandian** *(The Exploits of Esplandian)* described a beautiful island ruled by a pagan queen. Part of that book follows:

> *Know ye that at the right hand of the Indies there is an island named California, very close to that part of the Terrestrial Paradise, which is inhabited by black women, without a single man among them, and they lived in the manner of Amazons. They were robust of body, with strong and passionate hearts and great virtues. The island itself is one of the wildest in the world on account of the bold and craggy rocks. Their weapons were all made of gold. The island everywhere abounds with gold and precious stones, and upon it no other metal was found.*

The book was very popular when Cortes was exploring and conquering Mexico; it is likely that he and his men had read the story. Cortes himself wrote sometime after 1521 to his Spanish king about a rumored "Island of Amazons of women only, abounding in pearls and gold. . ." The fact that Baja is located across the Gulf of California west of Mexico contributed to the island myth. In meeting with the Colima Indians of Mexico, Cortes heard rumors of pearls to the west across the water. The island myth was disproven in 1539, when Francisco de Ulloa was sent by Cortes to encircle the "island" and to find the passage to the Far East. de Ulloa sailed to the north end of the Gulf of California and located the mouth of the Colorado River *(which he thought was the possible passage east)*. Although this expedition returned to the Mexican mainland, the official records of de Ulloa's trip were lost for 100 years. The myth continued; and until the mid-1700's California was still drawn as an island by most cartographers.

The exploration and settlement of Baja began in earnest in 1533, when two ships financed by Cortes went in search of the rumored pearls. The Indians of Baja were not usually friendly to the Spanish military and hostilities occurred. After 164 years of sporadic attempts to settle and Christianize the natives, the Spanish government decided that it had neither the men nor arms in Mexico to conquer the tribes by force. The Jesuit Order of Catholic priests was assigned the project. In 1697, under the leadership of padres Kino and Salvatierra, the missioning period of Baja started. A third priest, Father Ugarte, arranged financing for the Missions. Ugarte developed the Pious Fund as a means for collecting donations for the Baja Missions. From this money, the Alta California Missions were also financed.

The Indians of Baja used the available resources provided by nature for food, clothing, and shelter — the three basic needs for human survival. The men dressed scantily, if at all; but the women wore woven skirts of grasses or twigs. Some used animal hides for clothing and decorated the buckskins with bright painted figures, using a mixture of clays and the oils of crushed worms. Half capes of skins or bird feathers were also worn. The northern Baja Indians used pottery for cooking and storing water, while those farther south used tightly woven baskets. Putting small amounts of food and hot coals or rocks into a basket and shaking vigorously was a method of roasting nuts and seeds without burning the containers. Nuts and seeds were ground and crushed using metates found elsewhere among Mexican Indians. These people were hunters as well as gatherers of nuts, seeds and berries. Hardwood spears, and bows and arrows with points of chipped stone were made from native materials. The southern tribes had a type of blowgun made from reeds found around water

pools. "Yerba de la fleche" *(herb of the arrow)* was not used on arrowheads by Baja Indians as it was on the mainland. It did grow in southern Baja, however, and was respected for its poisonous qualities. The Baja tribes built shelters of native woods, reeds and stones. Most lived communally in large thatched houses, with open sides for ventilation in the tropical desert climate.

The Jesuits had a difficult time establishing permanent Mission sites. The nature of the desert soils and the scarcity of water posed the greatest limitations. Most of the tribes responded warmly to the kindness and direction offered by the padres. As in Alta California, the Spaniards brought changes to the land and the people of Baja. They grew wheat, cotton, grapes and other crops in the arid soils. The Indians were introduced to new food sources, new forms of shelters, new types of clothing, and new diseases. Smallpox, dysentery and measles killed thousands of natives, for they had no immunities to the Europeans' illnesses. Drought contributed to the weakened conditions of the Indians, and many ate locusts as their major food source during some especially dry years. During the smallpox epidemics of 1742, 1744, and 1748, it is estimated that over eighty percent of the total Indian population perished. In 1500, approximately 40,000 to 50,000 Indians lived on the peninsula. By 1800 the population had been reduced to about 5,000.

All of the Jesuit priests left in February 1768; but between 1697, when the first Mission at Loreto was dedicated, and 1768, the Order had founded twenty Missions. These Missions proved to be important supply stations for expeditions sent later to Alta California. The Jesuits were replaced by the Franciscan Order who continued the missioning of Baja. In 1773, the Franciscans relinquished the duties of Baja missioning to the Dominican Order. The Dominicans had requested royal permission to establish Missions. Father Serra, as Mission president, did not feel there was adequate land or population capacity to support two priestly orders. On Serra's recommendation, the Dominicans were given administrative control of Baja and the Franciscans Alta California. Thus, California was divided into two separate parts not only by name and administrative regions *(Baja versus Alta California)* but also as clergical districts.

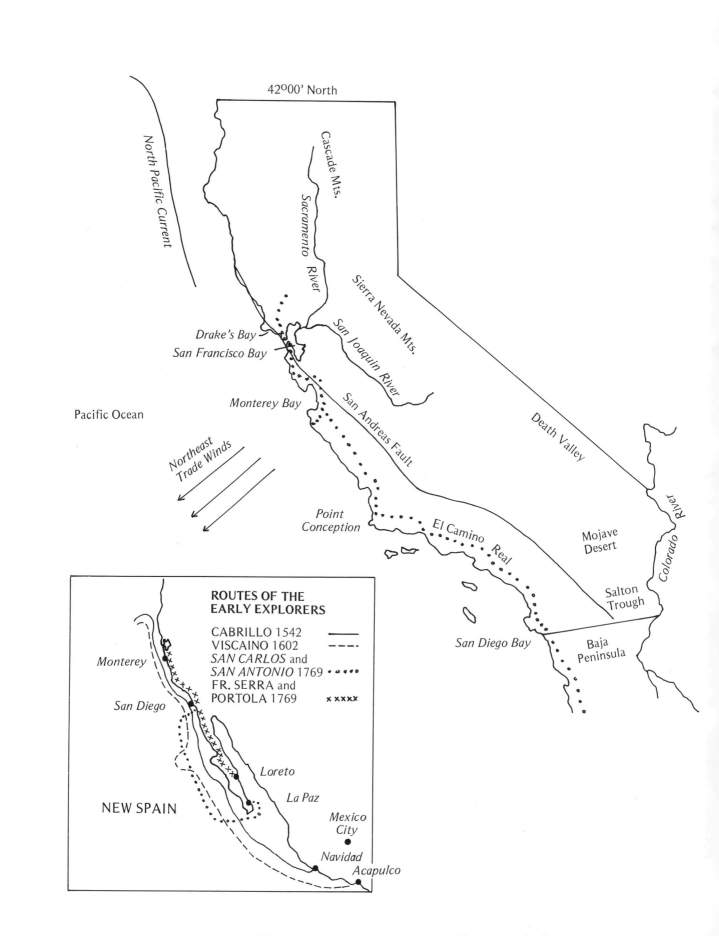

42°00' North

North Pacific Current

Cascade Mts.

Sacramento River

Sierra Nevada Mts.

San Joaquin River

Drake's Bay

San Francisco Bay

Pacific Ocean

Monterey Bay

San Andreas Fault

Death Valley

Northeast Trade Winds

Point Conception

El Camino Real

Mojave Desert

Salton Trough

Colorado River

San Diego Bay

Baja Peninsula

ROUTES OF THE EARLY EXPLORERS

CABRILLO 1542 ——————
VISCAINO 1602 — — — —
SAN CARLOS and
SAN ANTONIO 1769 • • • • •
FR. SERRA and
PORTOLA 1769 × × × × ×

Monterey

San Diego

Loreto

La Paz

Mexico City

NEW SPAIN

Navidad

Acapulco

Father Junipero Serra arrived in Baja to direct the Franciscan Missions there in 1768. He stayed but one year, for in 1769 his Order was given the authority to found a line of Missions with accompanying presidios in Alta California. The plan had two purposes:

1) to convert the Indians of Alta California to Christianity as loyal subjects of Spain; and

2) to prevent further southward progress of Russian fur trappers and settlers who were in the area just north of San Francisco Bay.

Between 1740 and 1765, Russians traveled the northern waters of the Pacific and settled several sites along the coasts and islands. King Carlos II of Spain was afraid of losing his claims in Alta California and of pirating of the Manilla galleons.

Two sea and land expeditions were launched which were to meet together and establish the first permanent Spanish settlement at San Diego Bay. The initial ship, the *San Carlos*, left La Paz, Baja, on January 7, 1769, with soldiers and supplies. It did not reach its destination for 110 days as the Northeast Trade Winds blew the ship 200 leagues off course. The *San Antonio* dropped anchor in the bay first, although it, like the *San Carlos*, had faulty maps which placed San Diego Bay 100 miles north of its actual location. The first land expedition left El Rosario Mission during the spring of 1769. This group reached San Diego Bay after a grueling two month, 350 mile trek north up the Baja peninsula. Father Crespi in his extensive diary described the land as "sterile, arid, lacking grass and water, and abounding in stones and thorns." They had started with a supply train comprised of 180 mules and 500 domestic animals and were accompanied by soldiers and Indian converts. Most of the Indians died or deserted along the trip. The second land group left Baja in mid-May 1769. Father Serra and Captain Portola, the military governor, were the leaders of this fourth expedition. They visited the existing Missions enroute and gathered supplies from them. Portola wrote, "I was obliged to seize everything I saw as I passed through those poor Missions, leaving them, to my keen regret, scantily provided for." Even so, the men ran out of food.

On July 1, 1769, the Spaniards were finally united; but they were in a sorry condition. For example, of the original crew of twenty-eight on the *San Antonio*, only eight survived the outward cruise to San Diego Bay. Of that eight, only two were alive when the ship returned to Baja to report the experiences and conditions of the San Diego unit and to gather more supplies. Of the 219 persons in the four expeditions that had ventured north, one-fourth died and another one-fourth deserted.

After a few days rest at San Diego Bay, Portola and a small company of soldiers went overland in search of Monterey Bay. Seeking the sheltered harbor described by Viscaino in 1602, Portola instead found the open arc of coastline thirty-eight days later. His party continued northward and came upon San Francisco Bay quite by surprise. Portola believed the body of water was an arm of the ocean and not a true bay. At that time, the present known Drake's Bay was called San Francisco Bay, having been named such in 1597 by another Spanish expedition. Portola realized by latitudinal means that his group had traveled too far north; and so they returned south without exploring the San Francisco Bay area. *(Later, two expeditions were sent to explore the area, and San Francisco Bay was described as large enough to "hold all the ships of Spain.")* Believing his party had never located Viscaino's discovery, Portola raised a cross anyway at the Monterey Bay shoreline and another near present day Carmel before returning to San Diego.

Shortly after Portola had left on that excursion, Father Serra erected a cross on the site of the first Mission in Alta California, San Diego de Alcala. Those persons who were able to work immediately began building a permanent shelter. San Diego de Alcala was short on provisions and was virtually a hospital for the ill and starving. Seven months later, more supplies arrived to save the dwindling band of Mission founders. In May 1770, a land and a sea group went to Monterey Bay to officially found the second Mission. On June 3, 1770, mass was celebrated and an altar erected under the same oak tree that Viscaino had used for services 168 years earlier. The Mission of San Carlos Borromeo de Carmelo was dedicated and the lands ceremoniously claimed for Spain.

A formidable geographic problem was distance, not only the 650 miles between San Diego and Monterey Bays, but also the great distance to Mexico for supplies. The Indian population, though usually friendly, was uncertain, suspicious, and occasionally hostile to the Spaniards. Self-sufficiency of the Missions required a large native population to plant and harvest the crops, tend to the livestock and make the necessary clothes, shelters and barter goods. According to Father Serra's plan, the answer was to build more Missions as a supply line and interdependent network.

For several years the missionaries rationed their goods, awaiting the infrequent mule trains and ships from Mexico. The route through Baja was mountainous desert much of the way, without reliable water and grass for the pack animals. A safer overland route was not mapped until 1774. Cargo ships were the primary supply source, but these were small craft and often delayed by storms and the Northeast Trade Winds or were simply lost at sea.

The first supply ship delegated to the San Diego Mission was the *San Jose.* It set sail in June 1769 from Baja; but after three months at sea and never reaching its destination, it returned to its home port. The *San Jose* sailed again towards the north in the spring of 1770, loaded with wines, dried meats, fruits, fish, beans, and supplies for the clergymen. The needed goods never arrived in Alta California, for the *San Jose* was lost at sea.

In addition to the danger of storms, misguided navigation, prevailing winds, and failing ships, the sailors of the 18th century faced the fear of scurvy's debilitating effects upon their health.

A problem of distance on a smaller scale was that of keeping the Indians and military men apart. The military believed that the Indians would not be peaceful and receptive to the Spaniards forever, and that defense was important to the success of each Mission. Therefore, the presidios and Missions should be placed close to each other for protection. Many of the Spanish guards were brutish convicts, however, and caused concern to the padres for the Indians' safety. For this reason the Mission at San Diego was moved in 1774, six miles upriver from its original site; and Monterey's Mission was relocated five miles away in 1771 to a location on the Carmel River.

New Missions were founded as supplies, soldiers and padres became available. The earlier ones were sited near the coastline, being dependent on ships for supplies. The Mission line grew northward from San Diego and southward from Monterey. San Francisco Bay, "formally" discovered shortly after 1770, was recognized for strategic purposes and two sites were developed there. Eventually the gap between the northern and southern clusters was closed, each Mission being approximately one long day's journey apart on the El Camino Real. With donations from existing Missions the later ones were not so dependent upon the sea and were built farther inland. None of the Missions were eastward of the coastal ranges and fertile valleys that divide those mountains. Plans were made and sites chosen for a second chain of Missions in the Central Valley of Alta California; however, this second line was never developed. Secularization of Alta California was ordered in 1834, ending the missioning period of that region.

Father Serra established nine Missions while president of the Alta California crusade. He was followed by Father Lasuen who also dedicated nine Missions. Three more were built before secularization. Mexico declared its independence from Spain in 1810, and the government desired to pursue the traditional plan of secularization. In theory a Mission was founded as a self-sufficient frontier post with its term of life a temporary ten years. At the end of that time, the natives were to be able to govern a pueblo, subject to civil laws, and the Mission church was to be given to the regular clergy. In California the term was sixty-five years, as the Indians, wrenched from their Stone Age culture into 18th century demands, were not ready to manage or support their own political and religious affairs at the end of the traditional ten year period.

Missioning was an inexpensive and economical colonial enterprise. One or two priests, a small number of soldiers, and a load of supplies formed the basis of a permanent settlement. Funding was provided by the Pious Fund, and each Mission was given $1000 to purchase bells, tools, seeds, and other necessities that could not be found or easily made at the Mission site. Established Missions were expected to donate vine cuttings, livestock and other items that might be spared. No properties were owned by the padres; all lands belonged to the Spanish — and later, Mexican-government,held in stewardship by the padres for the Indians.

The priestly duties were exhausting and had far reaching effects upon California's heritage. In addition to religious instruction, the padres were to

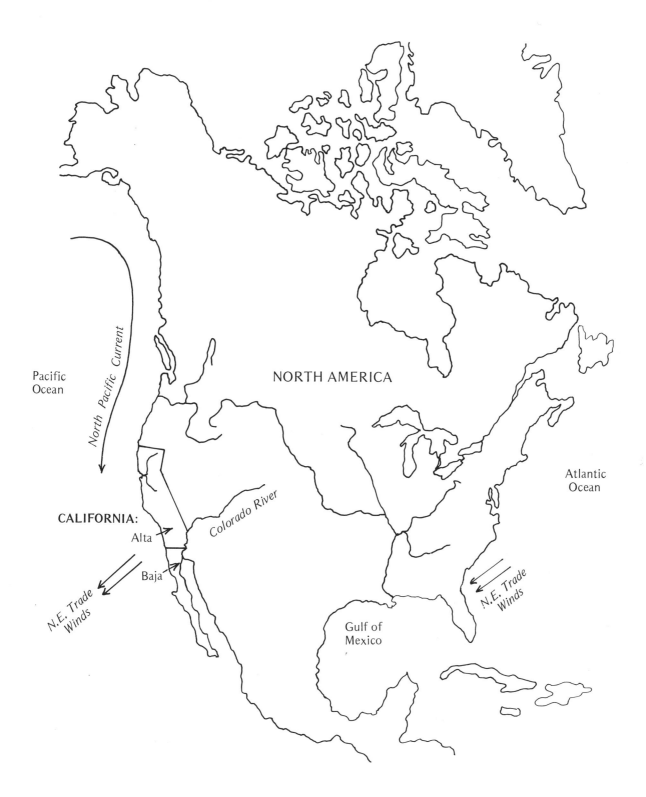

Pacific
Ocean

North Pacific Current

NORTH AMERICA

Atlantic
Ocean

CALIFORNIA:

Alta

Colorado River

Baja

N.E. Trade
Winds

N.E. Trade
Winds

Gulf of
Mexico

educate the natives, oversee the growing of crops and raising of livestock, and teach skills such as saddlemaking, weaving and winemaking. Few Indians were ever taught to read or write, as existence of Mission life warranted that agricultural and industrial skills be the primary goals. The Missions also entered into business transactions by bartering their produce to one another and to the ships, traders, and fur trappers that visited.

At the time of secularization in 1834, when control of the Missions and their properties were released to the natives and sold or gambled to Spaniards for ranchos, the Missions herded 396,000 cattle, 62,000 horses, and 321,000 hogs, sheep and goats. Also that year, the Indians harvested 123,000 bushels of grain. These are indeed remarkable achievements, for there was not a cow, horse, sheep, goat, hog, or grain of wheat in Alta California in 1769. Resulting from the array of priestly duties, California has inherited the Spanish language and place names, house and town architectural styles, agricultural crops and hydrologic knowledge, ranching techniques and animal husbandry, transportation routes such as the El Camino Real *(the first highway of California)*, and an appreciation for the inter-workings of sea, land, and climate.

The Relationships Between Physical Geography and Human Settlements

A basic knowledge of physical geography is important to understand how man lives within a region, in this case Baja and Alta California. Geography is the science of place study and the relationships and interactions between places. "Where" is the first question a geographer asks. Physical geography is the study of natural forms *(not man-made things)* found on the face of the earth, forms such as mountains, oceans, deserts, minerals, climates, soils, plants, etc. Settlement geography is the study of human sites, where they are placed and how man relates and interacts with the natural environment. Baja and Alta California, when examined as one regional unit, has five major areas of landscapes and four major areas of climate.

These determine the types of soils found in each area, which in turn determine what types of plants may grow in each area. Human and animal life is also governed by these same factors. How man dresses, what he eats, what kinds of shelters he builds, what jobs he does, how he lives — today or

as California Indians centuries ago — are influenced by the landscape and climate. Man, with some limitations, may alter the provisions of his environment according to his wishes and desires and his accumulating scientific knowledge. Remember, however, that the Missions of the 18th century were basically self-sufficient units and were dependent upon the environment as nature provided.

The missionaries, sailors and soldiers who founded the Missions of California were courageous for leaving the safety of the harbor ports and towns of Mexico. They examined the landscape, ocean and streams, weather, flora and fauna as they traveled north and wrote their observations in ships' logs and diaries, and in letters to their kings, generals, and Church fathers.

If an area looked much like their homeland of Spain, it was valued as an area more easily settled than an area different from their homeland. Conclusions were established that formed the basis for the future use of an area. For example, Viscaino's description of Monterey Bay misled Portola's expedition, for it was seeking a sheltered harbor, which Monterey Bay is not; yet Portola and Father Serra established the second mission site at that bay, bypassing the shelter and strategic importance of San Francisco Bay. So the natural forms, or physical geography, of Baja and Alta California and their interactions with man are important in the study of California's missioning period.

Baja and Alta California make up part of the western mountainous edge of the North American continent. Stretching along the Pacific Ocean for 1650 miles between 23½ and 42 degrees north latitude, many highly varied landscapes and climates are found. "Microclimates" within the area have been identified; but this text will deal only with general climatic regions. In addition to the variety of landscapes and climates, California sits on the eastern arc of the "Pacific Ring of Fire", a ring around the Pacific Ocean marked by movement of the earth's crust, which produces earthquakes and volcanoes. The San Andreas Fault is evidence of the "Pacific Ring of Fire" in California. Vulcanism and faulting have produced much of the landscape, and present inhabitants of California, like the mission founders, are aware that changes caused by movement will continue.

PHYSIOGRAPHIC REGIONS
OF CALIFORNIA

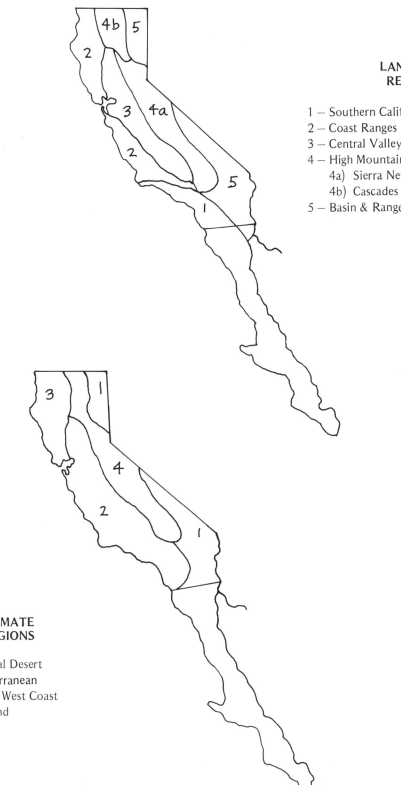

**LANDFORM
REGIONS**

1 — Southern California Mountains & Basins
2 — Coast Ranges
3 — Central Valley
4 — High Mountains
   4a) Sierra Nevadas
   4b) Cascades
5 — Basin & Range Country

**CLIMATE
REGIONS**

1 — Tropical Desert
2 — Mediterranean
3 — Marine West Coast
4 — Highland

As stated previously, California has five major areas of landscapes and four major areas of climate. The landscape areas are the

      1) Southern California Mountains and Basins;
      2) Coast Ranges;
      3) Central Valley;
      4) Sierra Nevada and Cascade Mountains; and
      5) Basin and Range Country.

The coastal mountains of the first area form an arc from Point Conception southward to the Mexican border and continue through the Baja peninsula. Although most of the mountains are less than 4,000 feet high, some reach over 10,000 feet. Between Los Angeles and San Diego, low steep valleys meet the ocean. The mountains have several good natural passage ways that have encouraged travel and settlement. Two of these are Cajon Pass and Ridge Route. East of these mountains lies the flat floor of the Salton Trough, a down-dropped basin of the earth's crust 235 feet below sea level.

The Coast Ranges run along the Pacific coastline in a parallel manner. Lower than the southern mountains, the ranges are divided by river valleys that lead to the Pacific. Each valley region encouraged separate settlements as small agricultural units. The coastline is often rugged and jagged where the land meets the sea. There is one large break in the Coast Ranges, San Francisco Bay, where the Pacific Ocean meets the Central Valley *(the third landscape area)*. The Sacramento and San Joaquin Rivers join together at this point and flow into the waters of the ocean.

The Central Valley is enclosed by the Coastal Ranges to the west and the high mountains to the east. Like the Coast Ranges, it also runs in a southeast to northwest direction. The northern border is marked by the Klamath Mountains separating California from Oregon. The southern end is closed by a transverse range extending east from the Coastal Ranges to meet the Sierra Nevadas. The Central Valley is a lowland filled with rich glacial soil deposits *(alluvium)* carried down from the towering Sierra Nevadas during the Ice Ages, making this region one of the world's finest for agricultural crops.

The Sierra Nevada and Cascade Mountains make up the fourth landscape area and are an impressive barrier to man's travels west to east across California. The Sierra Nevadas are a huge block of earth tilted to the west with a sharp drop on the eastern side. Few land routes cross this barrier, and there are no rivers crossing it in California. Faulting, the rising or sinking of the earth's surface, has been most severe along the south-eastern edge of this landform. The mountains were heavily glaciated, and a few small glaciers still remain in high, protected spots. The great glaciers gouged out jagged ridges and steep valleys on the eastern face of the Sierras and formed U-shaped valleys on the western side. Yosemite is one of these U-shaped valleys. The Cascade Mountains, unlike other ranges in California, were formed by volcanic activity and not by faulting. Lassen Peak and snow-capped Mount Shasta are part of the Cascade range.

The last landscape area is the Basin and Range Country. It is located to the east and south of the Sierra Nevada and Cascade Mountains. The southern section was formed by faulting of the earth in a north to south pattern with many down-dropped basins as the Sierras rose. Much of the northern section is a lava plateau, where thousands of years ago molten rock broke through the earth's crust and poured over the area. Windswept arid land is typical of the Basin and Range Country. Death Valley, the lowest point in North America at 282 feet below sea level, is one of the deserts found here.

The Basin and Range Country is the driest and hottest region of the United States, for the mountains block the moisture in the winds from the Pacific Ocean. This is called a rain-shadow effect, meaning that most moisture held in the winds falls on the windward side *(mountain side facing the ocean)*. When the winds rise up the windward side, they become heavy with water and drop this moisture in the forms of rain, snow, etc. As they cross over the peaks and descent the leeward side *(mountain side away from the ocean)*, the winds warm and dry out and do not release much moisture to the landscape.

Baja and Alta California have four major climate areas. Climate, a combination of weather forces, is the most critical physical force for determining and delineating an area. Climate is made up of temperature, precipitation, air pressure, prevailing winds, and storms that are found in an area. These weather forces are, in turn, influenced by the latitude of the area, altitude of the landforms, and large bodies of water nearby.

Over the surface of the earth there are many climate regions; but herein only four will be discussed that pertain to California. These four are the

1) Tropical Desert;
2) Mediterranean;
3) Marine West Coast;
   and
4) Highland.

All four climates are influenced by the cool waters of the Pacific Ocean and the prevailing winds, the Northeast Trades. The winds blow from northeast to southwest and were quite a hindrance to the early sailors of the California coasts. The ocean is the main source of water that is carried in the winds onto the bodies of land. The ocean waters heat and cool more slowly than does the land; this causes the sea waters to have an influence on the temperatures on the land nearby. The coastal regions have milder (temperate) climates with less extremes of hot or cold than do the regions farther inland from the oceans. San Francisco Bay, in addition to the Pacific coastline, has a tempering effect upon surrounding lands. Tule fog in the Central Valley is due to warm moist air moving inland off the Pacific and bay which meets the cooler landforms in the Central Valley.

Altitude influences climate in that as the higher one travels above sea level, the cooler the temperature. Air is cooled at the lapse rate of about 3.5 degrees Fahrenheit for each 1000 feet increase of elevation. Therefore, air is much cooler high in the mountains than at sea level. Mountains are a barrier to winds and force the winds to rise up the windward side, cooling as they rise. As air cools, its ability to hold water increases until it becomes so heavy that it may accumulate no more. This is called the dew point, the temperature at which the air is saturated. Clouds begin to form after the dew point is reached, and if the air continues to rise and cool, the water in the air will turn into droplets and fall as rain, snow, sleet, or hail. With this information, re-reading the section on the Basin and Range Country may give further understanding of the rain-shadow effect of mountain moisture.

The Tropical Desert climate of Baja and Alta California matches that of the Basin and Range Country and southern portions of the Coast Ranges. It is a land of sparse vegetation, sand dunes, and rocky soils. During the summer months, scorching temperatures are likely. Winter months are thirty to forty degrees cooler. The skies are usually cloudless, and this with the scant plan covering, means that the earth's surface heats very quickly during the day and cools quickly at night. It may be very hot in this climate during the day and feel cold at night. The land receives less than fifteen inches of moisture per year, most of it during the summer months. The plants and animals are well adapted to the climate. Cactus and other types of xerophytic plants that grow in the desert may be dormant for long periods of time and then suddenly bloom with a rainstorm or snow covering. At the southern tip of Baja there is a bit more moisture, up to twenty inches per year. The amount varies from year to year, however, and often caused the settlers and missionaries to continue farming the poor soils during a rainy year, only to have the crop fail for many dry years that followed.

The second climate region of Baja and Alta California is called Mediterranean. It is named this because the largest climate region of this type in the world is located around the Mediterranean Sea. It was a comfortable climate for the Spanish missionaries because it was like their homeland climate. This area covers the Central Valley and the northern Coast Ranges to San Francisco. The summer temperatures may be hot, but the winters are mild due to the ocean's tempering influence. The Mediterranean climate receives fifteen to twenty-five inches of moisture per year, most of it during the winter months. Many of the plants are desert types, especially in the southern portion of the area. Citrus fruits, olives, grapes, and other hardy food plants grow well. The soils may be fertile, exceptionally so in the Central Valley when irrigated by man. Much of this area was once pasture grasses, excellent for sheep, goats, horses, and cattle. These were the animals brought to California by the Spaniards. A severe seasonal problem indigenous to the Coast Ranges of this climate is the Santa Ana winds which sweep down the hills towards the sea in the dry months. Should fire accompany the winds, the hills may be stripped of natural vegetation and wildlife and homes; the soil is then exposed to wind and water erosion during the winter rainy season.

The Marine West Coast climate lies north of San Francisco Bay. It is also mild, but wetter and cooler than the Mediterranean region. Northern Spain has a similar climate area; so again, the missionaries felt "at home" in northern California. Large amounts of rainfall promote the growth of forests such as the California redwoods and oaks. The forests provided food and timber for the Indians and missionaries that inhabited this area. The skies are usually cloudy, making the day and night temperatures almost the same. Temperatures are generally mild with cool summers and winters just cold enough to produce a dormant period for plants. The area is humid and cloud covered with the dew point at maximum most of the time. This is excellent for plant growth. The amount of moisture per year varies according to the height of the mountains along the coast. In general, it may be noted that this climate area receives over twenty-five inches of moisture per year, increasing to great amounts the farther north of San Francisco one travels.

The last climate area is Highland, found in the Sierra Nevada and Cascade Mountains. Plant cover and moisture differ with the altitude, for the greater the elevation above sea level, the cooler the temperature and the greater the moisture amount. On the windward side of the mountains, small plants, grasses, bushes, and tall forest trees may be found. At the higher elevations, the trees become smaller, not due so much to lack of moisture, but more to the thinning of the soils, the cooling of the temperature, and the shortening of the grow-ing season. The trees are shorter and less dense as one climbs in altitude; short grasses become common at the timberline. Then the grasses give way to tiny mosses that cling to the poor soils and rocks at the highest levels. Because there is a rapid decrease of air pressure with an increase in eleva-tion, few settlements are sited at the highest altitudes. Sleeplessness, faintness, nausea, head-aches, and weakness may bother the mountain traveler. At the lower elevations less rainfall occurs as this climate region melds to the Mediterranean and Marine West Coast climates in the Central Valley. Moisture from the higher elevations, how-ever, runs down the mountain streams to the Central Valley for human, animal and plant use.

Conclusion

In order for the Missions to operate as self-sufficient units, the padres chose sites that were well endowed by nature. Missioning was more successful in Alta California than in Baja. The soils were more fertile, the water supply more dependable, and the Indians more docile. Missions were built in the Coastal Range landscape area of Alta California; and here the imported animals and plants adapted more easily to the climates than they did in the Tropical Desert climate of Baja. Nature provided well for the native population of Alta California as well. Animals and plants were available to the hunters and gatherers of food. A large population, the third determining factor of Mission location, was therefore supported by the abundant food supply. It is estimate that there were 180,000 to 250,000 natives in Alta California in 1769, one of the most densely populated Indian areas on the continent north of Mexico. The proximity to the Pacific Ocean of the Missions meant that the early sites could be serviced by supply ships from Mexico until self-sufficiency was possible.

As mentioned previously, a second chain of Missions was planned for the Central Valley. It would probably have succeeded as well as the first line of Missions. The three factors of site selection —arable soils, dependable water supplies, and a large local Indian population — would have been met in the Central Valley. Missioning was not possible on a large scale in the high mountains or the Basin and Range Country. Flora and fauna are plentiful in the mountains, but the struggle for winter provisions of food, clothing and shelter would have been great. Domesticated animals would need shelters in the areas of extreme snow-falls; and the lack of large pasture areas would not permit the growing of animal fodders and domestic grains in necessary amounts. The aridity of the land in the Basin and Range Country was the greatest hindrance there, as the lack of dependable water and rough soils made cultivation of crops difficult. There were large populations of Indians inhabiting this area, but they were generally not as friendly as the tribes to the west.

Overall, the Franciscans chose the best possible areas for missioning. Only in the Coastal Ranges, with their accompanying fertile river valleys, were all three factors of site selection readily met. The soils were easily cultivated for the growing of human crops and animals grasses. The water supply was dependable during the seasons for drinking consumption and irrigation use. The dense Indian population was receptive to the Spanish immigrants, and provided the missionaries with a labor force of religious converts. A visit to any of the California Missions is an invigorating step back in time and is recommended to all persons. Only then may one truly understand and appreciate how a small group of dedicated priests and soldiers made a tremendous impact upon the heritage of California.

A Note to Teachers and Parents

The following sections, *Activities and Glossary of Geographic Terms,* are oriented for anyone interested in the world around. Some may require level adjustments up or down according to individual needs. The glossary, as the reader will observe, contains many words that are not discussed in the content of this book. It has been designed to provide further insight to geographic studies that, hopefully, the teacher/parent will pursue with students.

The study of geography is often overlooked in the home and classroom — especially in the upper grades — for a variety of reasons. Instructors may be uncomfortable or unfamiliar with the curriculum and therefore not include a geography unit. Or they may believe that map exercises are busy work for young children and of no interest or concern as we grow up.

Geographic ignorance among all ages is a serious problem, particularly in light of the complex relationships of the twentieth century between regions due to economics and politics. Youngsters will advance in concrete and abstract knowledge with a progressive study of home, neighborhood, town, city and state. Through the teaching of geographic concepts, a child will learn what his/her needs are — both individual and cultural — and what the immediate natural environment provides or lacks. An awareness should develop that each person in a modern society is dependent and reliant upon many regions for fulfillment of those needs. In addition to an awareness of the geographic relationships, learners at home or school may be led in discussions of value clarification concerning human needs and wants. Noble goals are often difficult to achieve and sometimes frustrating; if, however, the incorporation of realistic geographic objectives is included in the social studies through the grade levels, our young people will be better informed adults in the end. And this is the ultimate aim of all educators.

Activities

No. 1 — Map Exercise "Trip Tic"

Using a road map, plan and draw your own "trip tic" to a California Mission. The American Automobile Association may provide a "trip tic" for use as an example. As you study the physiographic regions of the state, you can add pictures and information about the scenery you will see along the route to the Mission. Include not only information on the land, climate, wildlife and plants, but also highways, cities and towns, and the distances and time involved on the trip.

No. 2 — Graphs "Climatic Regions"

Choose one major city within each climate region of California for a comparative weather study. Construct a graph for each city (a total of four graphs) on separate posters. On the same day of each week, plot the high and low temperature recorded for each city. Use three colors: black (moisture), red (high temperature) and blue (low temperature) to connect the weekly readings. At the end of your study period, compare the temperature reports of the cities. What conclusions may be drawn about the weather similarities and differences between the study sites?

(This same exercise may be done in conjunction with precipitation graphs).

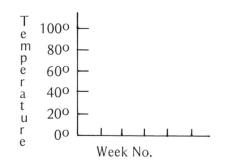

No. 3 — Map Exercise "City Planning"

Children draw four square blocks of a town — perhaps their own — on blank paper. Things to consider: roads, intersections, traffic flows, residential areas, commercial districts, numbering of blocks and buildings, schools, recreation areas, etc. Emphasize needs of community as well as child's familiarity with his/her own needs.

Maps will reflect age level and mobility of students. Groups could then join maps together — somewhat like developers do — and project the workings of the town.

No. 4 — Map Exercise "My Home Town"

By study of local town/city development, begin a class map of the home town core. Start with the earliest streets plotted, business and homes on those streets. Limit the area to several blocks according to study level of students. Direction of growth, usage and changes of the study area should be emphasized. Why and how has the town core been altered?

Libraries, personal interviews with senior citizens, private picture collections, etc., are excellent sources of information.

No. 5 — Glossary — "Geography Dictionary"

During study of California's Missions, students compile a list of geographic terms. Do not give these in alphabetical order, for that is part of the exercise. Students make a dictionary, alphabetizing, defining and using each word as it
a) relates to the study of the Missions;
b) to their own community and
c) to their own experiences.

In addition, children could be asked to illustrate each term.

For example:
elevation — height above the surface of the earth.

a) The California Missions are not located at high elevations in the Sierra Nevada Mountains.

b) The elevation of my town/city is 1000 feet above sea level.

c) I visited Carmel on vacation, and the elevation there is at sea level where the Pacific Ocean meets the shoreline.

d)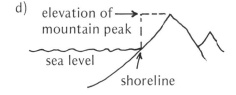

No. 6 — Picture Study "Regions of California"

Make a scrapbook or bulletin board display of pictures depicting the land-form and climate regions of California. Pictures may reflect natural scenery as well as urban development. This same activity works well on a mural map of the state.

No. 7 — Mural "Life in California: Then and Now"

As a class project or individual study, students draw a large map of the state. Personal drawings or pasted pictures may be used to depict the way of life across the state.

No. 8 — Mural "Along the El Camino Real"

On a large mural of Alta and Baja California, draw the route of the El Camino Real. Add Mission sites, names, dates of foundings, etc. Suggested pictures include Indian way of life in the 1700's, arrival of the Spanish and the introduction of crops, live-stock, buildings and ships brought by the immigrants.

No. 9 — Writing Time: "Cabrillo's Log"

Participants make a ship's log as if they were Cabrillo sailing the California coast-line in 1542. Imagination is good, but base story of daily/weekly entries on historic facts of the voyage. Persons may draw maps as part of their entries. Notes could include life on the ship, navigation tools, ocean winds and currents, shoreline scenery, etc. An excellent outgrowth of this would be a class play.

No. 10 — Writing Time: "Awaiting the Muletrain"

As a padre at a Spanish Mission, have students diarize a day in the life of a padre. Note in what skills the padre instruct the Indians, and agricultural needs of the Missions. How and where was water obtained, channeled and stored during the summer dry season? From where and how often did supplies arrive from Mexico? What items could be produced at the site and what items were imported?

No. 11 — Writing Exercise: "Tools of the Missionaries"

Girls and boys compare availability and usage of tools at the Missions for agricultural production compared with the farmers' needs today. Emphasize simplicity of 1700's life and self-sufficiency versus the economics of the 20th century farmer/rancher.

A visit to an agricultural museum is recommended, as well as antique stores, old garages and barns. The class could start a tool collection for their school or town.

Write a Mission Report

<u>Outline</u>

I. Founding
    A. Father Serra
    B. Father Lasuén
    C. Indians

II. The First buildings
    A. Materials used
    B. Plan for the buildings

III. Early years at the Mission
    A. The big fire
    B. Rebuilding of the church

IV. The Indians
    A. What tribes
    B. Their houses, jobs and skills

V. The mission irrigation
    A. Fountains
    B. Ditches

VI. Jobs for the Padres at the mission
    A. Livestock
    B. Crops
    C. Education of Indians
    D. Record keeping

Glossary of Geographic Terms

acclimate — to accustom or become accustomed to a different climate or environment.

air mass — an extensive portion of the atmosphere that is relatively homogenous as to temperature, humidity, and other factors.

alluvium — a deposit of earth materials left by water flowing over land not permanently submerged.

altitude — the height of a thing above the surface of the earth or above sea level.

antarctic — region of the earth of or near the South Pole.

Antarctic Circle — an imaginary circle parallel to the equator, 66 degrees 33 minutes south of it.

arable — region of the earth of or near the North Pole.

Arctic Circle — an imaginary circle parallel to the equator, 66 degrees 33 minutes north of it.

arid — lacking enough water for things to grow; dry and barren.

atmosphere — the gaseous envelope surrounding the earth consisting of oxygen, nitrogen, and other gases extending to an altitude of about 22,000 miles and rotating with the earth.

atmospheric pressure — the mass weight of a column of air above a given point.

axis — the imaginary straight line extending between the North and South Poles on which the earth rotates.

basin — a wide depressed area of the earth's surface in which the rock layers all incline towards the center.

bay — a part of a sea or lake indenting the shore line; wide inlet not so large as a gulf.

cartography — the art or work of making maps.

circle of illumination — the line which separates day from night on the earth due to rotation of the earth on its axis.

cliff — high, steep face of rock, especially one on a coast.

climate — the average conditions of weather at a particular place.

climatic controls — elements influencing climate, such as latitude, land and water, altitude, winds, mountain barriers, ocean currents, and air masses.

climatic region — any portion of the earth's surface over which the climatic elements are similar.

cloud — a visible mass of condensed water vapor suspended in the atmosphere, consisting of minute droplets or ice crystals, commonly classified in four groups: high clouds above 20,000 feet, intermediate clouds 6,500 to 20,000 feet, low clouds below 6,500 feet, and clouds of great vertical continuity.

coast — land alongside the sea; seashore.

cold front — a steep frontal surface between a confrontation of two masses of air in which the cold air is displacing the warmer air.

continent — any of the main large land areas of the earth, conventionally regarded *(with or without outlying islands)* as units: Africa, Asia, Australia, Europe, North America, South America, Antarctica.

crust (earth) — the solid, rocky, outer portion or shell of the earth; lithosphere.

current (water; air) — a flow of water or air, especially when strong or swift in a definite direction; specifically, such a flow within a larger body of water or mass of air.

delta — a deposit of sand and soil, usually triangular, formed at the mouth of some rivers.

demography — the statistical science dealing with the distribution, density, vital statistics, etc. of populations.

desert — a dry, barren, sandy region, naturally incapable of supporting almots any plant or animal life.

dew point — air temperature at which the air is saturated with moisture and may hold no more.

direction — the point toward which something faces or the line along which something moves *(north, south, east, west, up, down).*

direction finder — a device on a map that indicates direction.

earth grid — an imaginary scheme of lines over the surface of the earth by means of which location and direction may be determined *(lines of longitude and latitude).*

east — the direction to the right of a person facing north; direction in which sunrise occurs; it is properly the point on the horizon at which the center of the sun rises at the equinox; the point on a compass at 90 degrees directly opposite west.

elevation — height above the surface of the earth.

equator — an imaginary line around the middle of the earth halfway between the North Pole and the South Pole; 0 degrees latitude.

equinox — the two days of the year *(March 21 and September 21)* when the sun's rays strike the equator vertically so that all places on the earth have equal days and nights.

erosion — the picking up and transportation of weathered material to a lower elevation.

evaporate — to change a liquid or solid into vapor; to remove moisture from by heating or drying.

fault — a fracture in the earth's crust along which there has been displacement of the two sides in relation to each other.

fog — a large mass of water vapor condensed to fine particles, at or just above the earth's surface.

front — the surface boundary between two types of air masses.

geography — the descriptive science dealing with the surface of the earth, its division into continents and countries, and the climate, plants, animals, natural resources, inhabitants, and industries of the various divisions; the study of interactions between atmosphere, lithosphere and hydrosphere.

glacier — a large mass of ice and snow that forms in areas where the rate of snowfall constantly exceeds the rate at which the snow melts; it moves slowly outward from the center of accumulation or down a mountain slope or valley until it melts or breaks away.

great circle — the largest circumference of the earth that can be drawn *(equator).*

growing season — the number of days when the weather is warm enough for crops to grow without damage from frost.

gulf — a large area of ocean, larger than a bay, reaching into land.

harbor — a protected inlet, or branch of a sea, lake, etc. used as a shelter and anchorage for ships.

hemisphere — any of the halves of the earth: the earth is divided by the equator into the Northern and Southern Hemispheres, and by a meridian into the Eastern Hemisphere *(containing Europe, Asia, Africa and Australia)* and the Western Hemisphere *(containing the Americas and the islands of the Pacific).*

hill — a natural raised part of the earth's surface, often rounded and smaller than a mountain.

humidity — the amount or degree of moisture in the air.

hydrology — the science dealing with the waters of the earth, their distribution on the surface and underground, and the cycle involving evaporation, precipitation, flow to the seas, etc.

hydrosphere — the aqueous envelope of the earth, including the oceans, lakes, streams, and underground waters, and the aqueous vapors in the atmosphere.

inclination of the earth — the tilting of the axis of the earth, so that it lies at an angle of 23½ degrees to the vertical of the plane of the ecliptic.

inland — of, located in, or confined to the interior of a country or region; away from the coast or border.

insolation — the solar radiation received at the earth's surface.

international date line — the meridian at approximately 180 degrees longitude, internationally accepted as a date line where the new day begins first.

island — a land mass not as large as a continent surrounded by water.

jet stream — narrow bands of high velocity winds in the upper troposphere.

key (map) — the explanation on a map.

lake — an inland body of water, usually fresh, larger than a pool or pond, and generally formed by some obstruction in the course of flowing water.

lapse rate — the temperature decrease of air from 3.3 to 3.5 degrees for each 1,000 feet rise in elevation.

landform — any topographic feature of the earth's surface, as a plain, valley, hill, etc., caused by erosion, movement, or sedimentation.

landscape — an expanse of natural scenery seen by the eye in one view.

latitude — the measurement of distance north and south of the equator by the use of imaginary lines *(parallels)* equidistant apart. *(equator is 0 degrees latitude; North Pole is 90 degrees north latitude; South Pole is 90 degrees south latitude).*

lava — melted rock issuing from a volcano; such rock solidified by cooling.

leeward — in the direction towards which the winds blow; side away from the wind; opposite of windward.

lithosphere — the solid part of the earth; earth's crust.

longitude — the measurement of distance east and west of the prime meridian by the use of imaginary lines *(meridians)* not equidistant apart.

mainland — the principal land or largest part of a continent, as distinguished from a relatively small island or peninsula.

map — the representation of a position of the curved earth on a flat surface.

meridian — an imaginary line that connects points of the same longitude.

mesa — a broad, flat-topped, erosional remnant flanked on at least one side by a steep cliff.

meteorology — science of the atmosphere and atmospheric phenomena; study of weather and climate.

mountain — a natural raised part of the earth's surface, usually rising more or less abruptly, and larger than a hill.

mountain range — a series of connected mountains considered as a single system because of geographical proximity or common origin.

mouth *(river)* — the part of a river, stream, etc. where the water empties into another body of water.

north — direction to the right of a person facing sunset; direction of the North Pole from any other point on the earth's surface; the point on a compass at 0 degrees, directly opposite south.

North Pole — the northern end of the earth's axis, 90 degrees north latitude; one of only two points on the earth's surface through which all meridians pass.

ocean — the great body of salt water that covers approximately 71 percent of the surface of the earth; any of its five principal geographical divisions: Atlantic, Pacific, Indian, Arctic or Antarctic Ocean.

orbit *(earth)* — the path followed by the earth in its journey around sun.

parallel — an imaginary line connecting points of the same latitude.

parallelism of the axis — the parallel position of the axis of the earth, at any point of its orbit during its annual revolution, to its position at any other point in the orbit due to the fixed inclination of the earth.

plane of the ecliptic — an imaginary plane that passes through the sun and extends outward to all points on the earth's orbit.

physical geography — the study of the features and nature of the earth's solid surface and oceans, atmosphere and climate, distribution of plant and animal life, etc.

plateau — an elevated tract or more or less level land; mesa.

precipitation — moisture in the form of rain, snow, sleet, etc.; the amount of this.

prevailing wind — winds greater in strength, influence, or effect on an area.

prime meridian — an arbitrary meridian selected as a base line in order to measure longitude.

projection *(map)* — the representation of the curved earth on a flat surface.

rain-shadow — a region of little rainfall on the lee slopes of mountains whose windward slopes receive the rain.

relative humidity — the amount of moisture in the air as compared with the maximum abmount that the air could contain at the same temperature, expressed as a percentage.

relief — the difference in elevation between the highest and lowest points within a local region.

revolution *(earth)* — the annual movement of the earth around the sun, taking approximately 365 days.

river — a natural stream of water larger than a creek and emptying into an ocean, lake or another river.

rotation — the daily turning of the earth on its axis, taking 24 hours.

scale *(map)* — the ratio between the actual size of an area and its size on a map.

sea — the continuous marine water of the entire earth.

sea level — the mean level of the surface of the sea.

season — any of the four arbitrary divisions of the year, characterized chiefly by differences in temperature, precipitation, amount of daylight, and plant growth *(spring, summer, autumn, winter)*; seasons are reversed between the Northern and Southern Hemispheres due to inclination of the earth on its axis and revolution around the sun by the earth on its orbit.

sedimentation — the depositing of matter by wind or water.

settlement geography — the study of human sites on the earth's surface and the influencing factors pertaining to or resulting from those sites.

soil — the loose surface material of the earth in which plants grow.

solar system — the planets together with their satellites and all the other bodies that revolve around the sun.

solstices — the two days of the year *(June 21 and December 21)* when the vertical rays of the sun have migrated their greatest distance poleward, north or south.

source — the point from which a river or stream comes into existence or develops, i.e., a spring fountain or junction of two streams.

south — the direction to the left of a person facing the sunset; direction of the South Pole from any other point on the earth's surface; the point on a compass at 180 degrees, directly opposite north.

South Pole — the southern end of the earth's axis, 90 degrees south latitude; one of only two points on the earth's surface through which all meridians pass.

standard time — time based on zones of 15 degrees of longitude. The central meridian in each zone is taken as the basis for determining time within the entire zone.

storm — an atmospheric disturbance characterized by a strong wind, usually accompanied by rain, snow, sleet, or hail, and often, thunder and lightning.

stream — a current or flow of water, especially one running on the surface of the earth; a small river.

temperature — the degree of heat of the atmosphere.

temperature inversion — an increase in temperature with a rise of altitude, rather than the normal lapse rate; occurs when warmer air overlies colder air.

timberline — the line above or beyond which trees do not grow, as on mountains or in polar regions.

topography — the science of drawing on maps and charts or otherwise representing the surface features of a region, including its relief and rivers, lakes, etc., and such man-made features as canals, bridges, roads, etc.

trade winds — constant easterly winds blowing equatorward from the subtropical high pressures to the equatorial doldrums.

transverse range — a mountain range lying crosswise and not with the surrounding direction of landforms.

tropics — the region of the earth lying between 23½ degrees north latitude and 23½ degrees south latitude, which mark the limits of the migration of the sun's vertical rays north and south due to the inclination of the earth's axis and to the earth's revolution.

Tropic of Cancer — the parallel 23½ degrees north of the equator which is the northermost distance that the sun's rays strike vertically in the Northern Hemisphere.

Tropic of Capricorn — the parallel 23½ degrees south of the equator which is the southermost distance that the sun's rays strike vertically in the Southern Hemisphere.

valley — a stretch of low land lying between hills or mountains and usually having a river or stream flowing through it.

volcano — a vent in the earth's crust through which molten rock, rock fragments, gases, ashes, etc. are ejected from the earth's interior: three classifications are 1) *active* while erupting, 2) *dormant* during a long period of inactivity, or 3) *extinct* when all activity has finally ceased.

vulcanism — the process which involves either a transfer of liquid from one place to another within the earth or its extrusion onto the surface.

warm front — the gentle surface between a confrontation of two masses of air in which the warm air rises over the cold air.

weather — the condition of the atmosphere as to temperature, pressure, humidity, and other meteorological phenomena at any given instant.

west — the direction to the left of a person facing north; direction in which sunset occurs; it is properly the point on the horizon at which the sun sits at the equinox; the point on a compass at 270 degrees directly opposite east.

windward — the direction or side from which the wind blows; side facing the wind; opposite of leeward.

xerophyte — that category of plants that are adapted to day conditions.

Suggested Readings

Griffin, Paul F.; Chatham, Ronald L.; and Young, Roubert N. *Anglo-America: a Systematic and Regional Geography.* 2nd Ed. Palo Alto, CA: Fearon Publishers. 1968.

Hoyt, Joseph Bixby. *Man and the Earth.* 3rd Ed. Englewood Cliffs, NJ: Prentice-Hall, Inc. 1973.

Miller, E. Willard, and Langdon, George. *Exploring Earth Environments.* New York, NY: Thomas Y. Crowell Company. 1964.

Paterson, J.H. *North America: a Geography of Canada and the United States.* 6th Ed. New York, NY: Oxford University Press. 1979.

Starkey, Otis P.; Robinson, J. Lewis; and Miller, Crane S. *The Anglo-American Realm.* 2nd Ed. New York, NY: McGraw-Hill Book Company. 1969.

Thoman, Richard S. *The United States and Canada: Present and Future.* Columbus, OH: Charles E. Merrill Publishing Company. 1978.

Humanizing Historical Characters

PAPER BAG PUPPET

Use lunch-size paper bag for best hand manipulation.
The fold becomes the mouth.

Materials — Lunch bags
      — Scissors
      — Pretty scraps
      — Glue
      — Crayons
      — Pencils

"un CABALLO"

"UNA VACA"

SOCK PUPPET I

Cut toe out of socks.
Sew oval insert into toe area.
Decorate as shown in illustration.

SOCK PUPPET II

Stuff "foot" of socks.
Insert cardboard cylinder.
Tie or use rubber band to keep in place.
Decorate as shown in illustration.

Materials — Socks
— Scissors
— Decorative scraps
— Needle
— Thread
— Glue

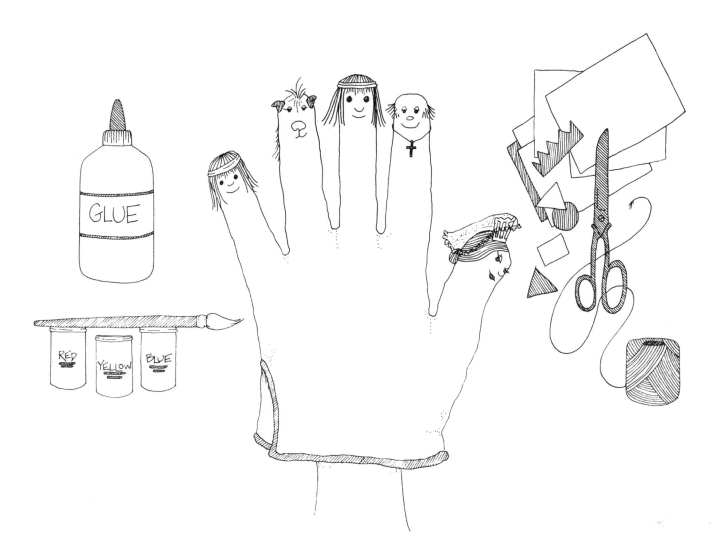

GLOVE FINGER PUPPET

Use a whole glove or cut off fingers of glove for a one-at-a-time puppet.

Materials — Cloth glove
            — Pretty scraps
            — Paint
            — Scissors
            — Glue

PAPER PLATE PUPPET

Fold a paper plate and staple in the center.
Fold and sew a large piece of cloth into a "sleeve"
and attach to the plate with glue or tape.
Finish and decorate.

Materials   — Bags
             — Scissors
             — Staples
             — Glue
             — Colored paper
             — Cloth
             — Needle and thread

LIGHT GLOBE PUPPET

Cover the light globe with vaseline; place in a paper
cylinder and onto the bottle for easy work. Build
up and strip with maché layers but don't cover the
bottle. Remove from the base. If you wish, remove
the glass by giving the head a hard crack then
carefully cutting the head and shaking the glass into
a bag. Retape head with maché or masking tape.
Decorate the puppet and dress it simply with paper
or cloth.

Materials — Glove
— Bottle
— Cylinder
— Maché mash and strips
— Decorative scraps
— Scissors
— Cloth
— Glue

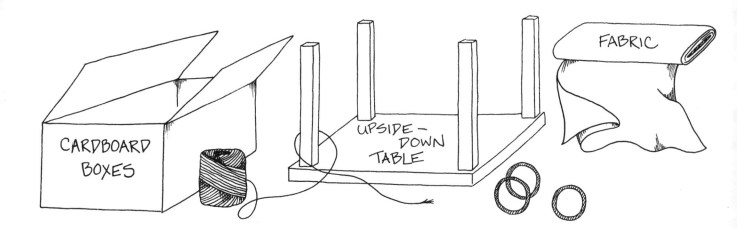

PUPPET STAGES

Make puppet stages using big boxes or upsidedown tables, as shown. Put on a bit of the play given here; better yet, write one of your own!

Materials
— Box or table
— Cloth

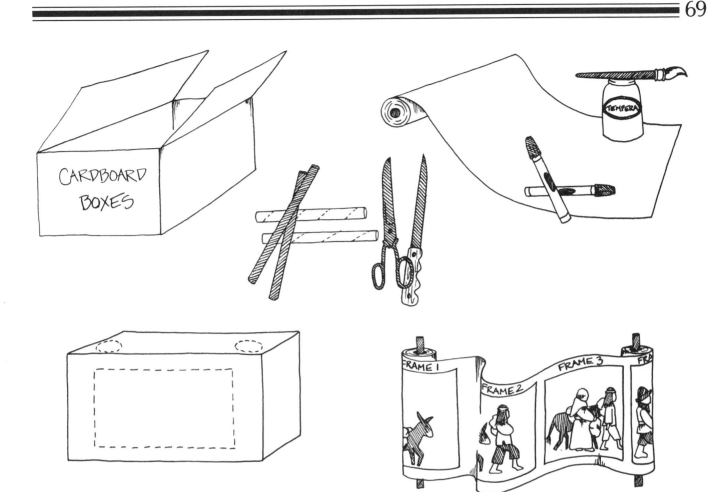

CREATE A MOVIE OR TELEVISION SHOW

Make the sequential story frames on a roll of shelf or cut down butcher paper. A cardboard box with a viewing hole cut in front and roling holes on top will work well. Dowel sticks cut taller than the box or cardboard cylinders make fine rollers.

Materials — Large box
— Dowel sticks
— Cardboard cylinders
— Shelf paper
— Paint or crayons or felt pen markers

PAPER PLATE MASK

Fasten string to each side of paper plate (as shown); decorate to give your desired personality to the mask.

Materials — Paper plate
           — String
           — Glue
           — Colored paper
           — Decorative scraps
           — Scissors
           — Paint

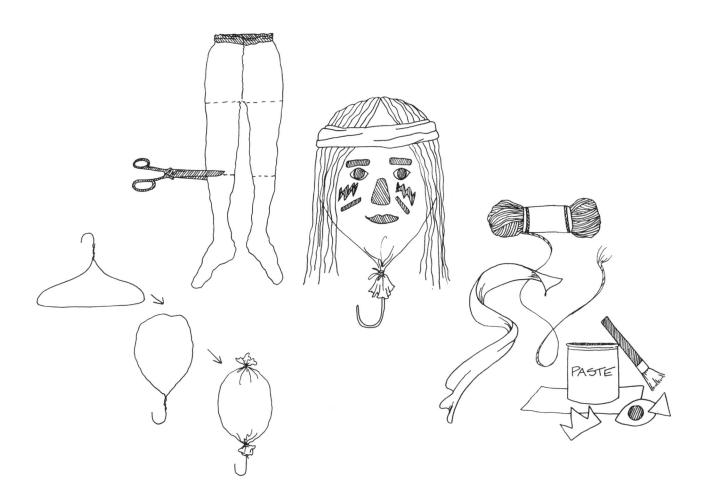

COAT HANGER MASK

Cut stocking off.
Shape wire coat hanger into a circle.
Stretch the stocking and tie as shown.
Decorate with paper and material.
Use it to hide behind.

Materials — Panty hose
— Wire hanger
— Decorative scraps
— Scissors
— Paste or glue

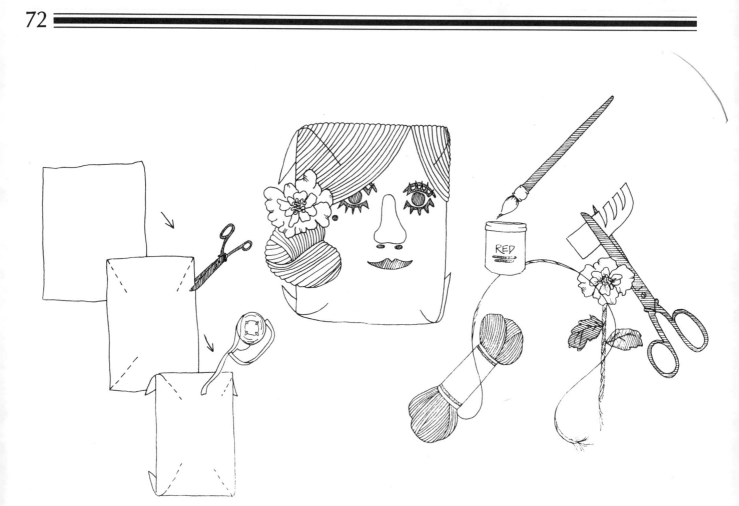

FOLDED PAPER MASK

Draw slashed lines.
Cut and tape as shown.
Use remaining lines as folding guides to give shape
to the mask.

Materials — Paper
— Scissors
— Decorative scraps
— Glue

The California Missions

INDIAN TRIBAL AREAS

1 ACHUMAWI	14 IPAI	34 POMO
2 ATSUGEWI	15 KAROK	35 SALINAN
3 CAHTO	16 KITANEMUK	36 SERRANO
4 CAHUILLA	17 KONKOW	37 SHASTA
5 CHEMEHUEVI	18 KOSO	38 SINKYONE
6 CHILULA	19 LASSIK	39 TATAVIAM
7 CHIMARIKO	20 LUISEÑO	40 TIPAI
8 CHUMASH	21 MAIDU	41 TOLOWA
9 COSTANOAN	22 MATTOLE	42 TUBATULABAL
10 CUPEÑO	23 MIWOK	43 VANYUMI
11 ESSELEN	24 MIWOK, COAST	44 WAILAKI
12 GABRIELINO	25 MIWOK, LAKE	45 WAPPO
13 HUPA	26 MODOC	46 WASHO
	27 MONACHE	47 WHILKUT
	28 MONO	48 WINTU
	29 NISENAN	49 WIYOT
	30 NOMLAKI	50 YANA
	31 NONGATL	51 YOKUTS, FOOTHILL
	32 PAIUTE	52 YOKUTS, NORTHERN
	33 PATWIN	53 YOKUTS, SOUTHERN (TULARE)
		54 YUKI
		55 YUROK

San Francisco Solano
San Rafael Arcángel
San Francisco de Asís
SAN FRANCISCO
San José de Guadalupe
Santa Clara de Asís
Santa Cruz
San Juan Bautista
MONTEREY
San Carlos Borroméo de Carmelo
Nuestra Señora de la Soledad
San Antonio de Padua
San Miguel Arcángel
San Luis Obispo de Tolosa
Santa Inés
La Purísima Concepción
Santa Barbara
San Buenaventura
SANTA BARBARA
San Fernando Rey de España
San Gabriel Arcángel
LOS ANGELES
San Juan Capistrano
San Luis Rey de Francia
San Diego de Alcalá
SAN DIEGO

San Diego de Alcalá

(First Mission, July 16, 1769)

Our civilization in California was born with the founding of this Mission. Like most births, it wasn't easy. Two overland parties and three ships were sent from Lower California to "Occupy and fortify San Diego and Monterey for God and the King of Spain", as ordered by Carlos III. One ship disappeared in a trial voyage before the expedition even started. Another, the *San Carlos*, was blown off course and the crew incapacitated with scurvy before they reached San Diego harbor. The overland parties tried to take too much livestock. Seeking water and grass took time making the journey long and hazardous.

The first few months in San Diego were even worse. Sickness, death, and near starvation reduced the survivors from about ninety to fewer than thirty.

The Indians did not appreciate that all of this was for their salvation. None were to be seen at the founding ceremonies. In the first year, not a single Indian was baptized. The Indians were at first shy but curious, then bolder to the extent they tried to steal everything except the food. They were afraid the food would make them sick like the white men.

In just a few years, the Fathers were converting enough Indians that the Indian leaders were afraid their tribal way of life would be destroyed. They plotted to drive the foreigners out of their land. On a dark night in November 1775, an army of hundreds of Indians attacked the Mission with spears, bows and arrows. Nine men and two boys were the entire white population at the Mission when the attack came. Father Luis Jayne rushed out to talk to the army. He was one of three defenders killed that night, the first Father martyred in California. The buildings were all burned. The Indians delayed the Mission movement with their attack but didn't drive it out.

The Mission prospered in the following years and had the fourth largest congregation in the Mission chain before secularization.

The present building was started in 1808. During secularization it fell into ruin, the roof was removed for the tile and the tower collapsed. Restoration started in 1896 and the church was re-dedicated in 1931. The restoration was guided by effect rather than accuracy, which left much to be desired. The most interesting feature of the church is the bell tower with five bells.

San Carlos Borromeo de Carmelo

(Second Mission, June 3, 1770)

Two days after he arrived at Monterey Bay, Father Serra consecrated the ground and celebrated mass under the same oak tree Viscaino used 168 years before. The natives were friendly. The natural beauty of the area and the climate all impressed Father Serra. This Mission became his headquarters for administration of the other Missions.

The first buildings were wooden structures because of the abundance of pine and cypress trees. However, the fathers were prompted to move the Mission away from the un-Christian conduct of the soldiers, to an area with more farm land at the mouth of Carmel Valley, its present location.

The first adobe church was started here in 1774, under the direction of Father Serra himself. The present stone church, a dream of Father Serra, was begun in 1793. Father Lasuen brought a master stone mason, Manuel Estevan Ruiz, from Mexico for the work. The Carmel area has a soft white stone that is easy to work. It hardens and turns a darker yellow when exposed to the air.

Although it was the administrative headquarters of the Missions it never had as many Indians as the others.

The architecture is more satisfying and unique than any in the Mission chain. The two towers are not "twin" but each very distinctive, one topped with a Moorish dome. The star window is simply fascinating.

In spite of its importance, religiously, architecturally and economically, it deteriorated rapidly after secularization. Before long it was a ruin. Attempts to restore it were started in 1881. A pitched roof was added to protect the walls but it was out of character with the architecture. In 1934, it was removed and an accurate restoration has taken place since.

The Mission at Carmel today is a parish church, and a visit to it is one of the great experiences we can have in reliving this part of our history.

San Antonio de Padua

(Third Mission, July 14, 1771)

If it weren't for the military presence in Hunter-Liggett, a visit to this Mission in a beautiful oak-studded valley in the Santa Lucia Mountains is almost like going back in time. Father Serra founded San Antonio on the route Portola took between San Diego and Monterey, the first Mission not on the coast.

The Indians were friendly, but were not too anxious to accept Christianity. However, the Mission continued to grow. An adobe chapel was built in 1782 with a tile roof. This is the first example of the use of the material that became a trade mark of Mission architecture to later generations.

Water was necessary before the Mission could really prosper, so eventually a complex water system that dammed the San Antonio River was developed. The system of reservoirs, settling ponds, and conduits were so well developed that the ranchers used them long after the Mission had fallen into ruin. A water-powered gristmill was built for grinding grain into flour that was justly famous throughout the Mission chain.

The present church was started in 1810. Its architecture is unusual and pleasing. It is an adobe building with a facade of decorative clay brick that also serves as a companario for three bells.

The Mission prospered until it counted 1,300 Indians and 17,491 head of livestock. After secularization, Governor Pio Pico offered to sell the disintegrated Mission but nobody wanted to buy it.

First attempts to restore the buildings began in 1903 but the earthquake of 1906 caused the project to be abandoned. Current restoration started in 1948 and is continuing.

San Gabriel Arcángel

(Fourth Mission, September 8, 1771)

Mission San Gabriel is completely surrounded by metropolitan growth. Where it is possible to visualize the third Mission, San Antonio, as it was in the eighteenth century, it is impossible with San Gabriel. Although the church building itself survived secularization and is in a more original condition than other Missions, you can not even imagine the vast agricultural lands controlled by the Mission.

There are several reasons for the success of San Gabriel. The Mission lands were very fertile, favored by a gentle climate and with available water. The fathers were hard working and resourceful over a period of time. The site was located at the cross-roads of three major land routes, from Mexico, from the east, and from the north.

The Indians were friendly until a soldier interrupted the harmony and a chief was killed. It took a while for the Fathers to reestablish a good feeling with the Indians. Eventually, the Mission was a spiritual and material success. It was so successful with agriculture products that it is known as the "Mother of California Agriculture".

The present church was begun in 1794, and finished in 1806. The thirty foot high walls are of stone to the windows, then of brick with stucco as the finish. The original roof was vaulted stone. An earthquake forced a change in design when the roof cracked and was replaced with a low pitched timber gable in 1803. Its unique Moorish design is inspired by the cathedral at Cordova, Spain where Father Cruzado had studied.

The prosperity and lands were lost during secularization but the church was never completely deserted. The United States restored the property to the Catholic Church with the church still intact. It served as a parish church from 1859 to 1908, when it was taken over by the Cloretan Fathers. It has been refurbished and had excellent care since that time.

San Luis Obispo de Tolosa

(Fifth Mission, September 1, 1772)

Father Serra founded this Mission while he was on his way to San Diego to hasten the supplies from Mexico aboard the ships to Monterey. He selected a site not on the coast, but several miles inland surrounded by mountains, known as the "Valley of the Bears". Portola had named the valley on his first trip to Monterey because of so many grizzly bears in the area.

At least three times in the first years of the Mission, these bears were used for food when provisions ran low. One hunt, from San Antonio and Carmel to save the starving people, produced over 9,000 lbs. of bear meat. No wonder the grizzly bears became extinct in California.

The Indians were friendly to the newcomers because they had also received meat from the bear hunts by trading seeds. They gave the Fathers food, but were not anxious to join the Mission because they had more food. It wasn't until the Mission began producing corn and beans that they attracted converts.

Wild Indians did attack the Mission on several occasions, enemies of some of the tribes who came to live there. They used burning arrows shot onto the thatched roofs, setting the buildings on fire. The Fathers were forced to make clay tile to roof the buildings. The idea was from San Antonio but before long it was used in all the Missions.

The present church was completed in 1793, an adobe building with a clay tile roof. The facade, with three bells, was not completed until 1820.

The Mission became a parish church after secularization and is still one. The adobe walls were covered with wood siding, the roof with wood shingles, and a wooden steeple was added to make it seem more like home to the settlers from the eastern United States. However, true restoration was started in 1933 to return it to its appearance today.

A city plaza has been developed in front of the church so the area is filled with activity as it was during its glory days.

San Francisco de Asís

(Sixth Mission, October 9, 1776)

The Great San Francisco Bay was rather late in being discovered because the Golden Gate is a narrow entrance for such a large bay. Portola finally determined it was a great bay on his second trip north. Its strategic importance was immediately recognized and orders were issued to found two Missions and a presidio with a colony of families there without delay.

Thus started one of the most remarkable overland treks in western history. Juan Bautista de Anza led 240 settlers and about 1,000 domestic animals from Sonora, Mexico, to Mission San Xavier del Bac, along the Gila River to the Colorado, forded it to cross the desert, the mountains, and the coastal plain to Mission San Gabriel. Then on to Monterey and finally arriving at San Francisco Bay. He arrived with four more people than he started, with new born babies.

The Mission was founded near a stream that Anza named Arroyo de los Dolores (Our Lady of Sorrows) because it was her feast day. Even today, the Mission is known as Mission Dolores rather than its official name.

The Mission grew slowly. The land was too sandy for good crops. The Indians appreciated the food, shelter, and protection of the Mission, but they were also influenced by the immoralities of the presidio and lack of discipline in their neighboring tribes. They ran away from the Mission in great numbers at times. Sickness was a major factor in limiting the Indian population of the Mission. Measles epidemics in 1806 and 1826 were responsible for over 500 Indian deaths. 5,500 Indians died here during the Mission's 58 years of existence.

The present church was dedicated in 1791, an adobe building with redwood roof timbers lashed together with rawhide, and clay tile roof. Redwood was available for construction from Monterey north. Wooden pegs of manzanita were commonly used to connect timbers in structures. The facade of the building was not built until about 1810 when skilled masons were available in the area.

After secularization, the church was used for various purposes so it didn't fall into ruin. The church has been carefully preserved and faithfully kept. It survived the great earthquake of 1906 and even in its City location, it has a distinctive character all its own even today.

San Juan de Capistrano

Deserts

Dry and inhospitable, the deserts of Baja prompted the missionaries to move north to Alta California.

Missions

Building models of the Missions is an excellent learning tool, and a picture is usually all that is needed.

Mountains

Watershed for the fertile valleys and plains below, the mountains provided abundant sources of fish and game for the Missions.

Tools

The Missions were well supplied with tools of the time for construction and food raising and processing.

Arts

Beautiful decorations of the Indians are a fine source of inspiration to young students.

Waters

Most of the Missions
developed by water
sources, either on the
coast or by streams
and lakes.

ADOBE BRICK MAKING

Indian Houses

Crafts

Children quickly become proficient in the crafts of the Spanish-California Mission era.

Valleys

Coastal valleys were the
location for most of the
Missions, well-watered
and very fertile.

San Juan de Capistrano

(Seventh Mission, November 1, 1776)

San Juan Capistrano was founded twice, the first time by Father Lasuen on October 30, 1775. Less than a week later, word arrived of the Indian uprising at San Diego. It was hastily abandoned and not founded again until Father Serra came a year later.

The Mission prospered immediately. The location near the sea had a mild climate, workable rich soil, water and friendly Indians. The Mission was the famous example of the hide and tallow trade that established a flourishing and profitable export to the eastern United States.

An adobe church was built, with the first section finished in 1777, a year after the founding of the Mission. It is the only one left existing in which Father Serra celebrated Mass.   To us it becomes important as the oldest building in California, and is known as "Father Serra's Chapel".

Beginning in 1796, work was started on a huge stone church to be the most impressive building in the whole Mission chain. Isidor Aguilar, an expert stonemason from Mexico, was brought to oversee the construction. The church was under construction for nine years. The immense structure had seven masonry domes, an unusually elaborate stone treatment, vaulting over the sanctuary, and side arches along the nave. It was a most sophisticated design and construction.

The church was used for only six years when the devastating earthquake of December 1812, toppled the tower and destroyed the church. Forty Indians were killed in the tragedy. It was never rebuilt.

In 1833, the Mission was secularized. The chapel was used for a time as a hay barn, thus the roof was maintained and the walls protected.

Attempts to restore the Mission started in 1860, but they mainly destroyed part of what was left. In 1920, a truly effective restoration started. Today this is a popular tourist attraction and the remains of the great stone church are resplendent, even in ruins.

Santa Clara de Asís

(Eighth Mission, January 12, 1777)

Santa Clara Mission was the second of the two ordered to be founded as protection for San Francisco Bay from the Russians or English. Some of the de Anza Colonists came to a new settlement nearby, the city of San Jose.

The site proved to be more difficult than ever imagined. At first, it was on the banks of the Guadalupe River, which flooded, two years later. It was moved to higher ground twice; then, in 1818, an earthquake destroyed the Mission. It was moved again, four times in all. The church was built and rebuilt a total of seven times, twice it was destroyed by fire.

In spite of these changing conditions, the Mission prospered and became one of the most successful in the whole chain of Missions. Santa Clara had very competent Fathers directing the Mission operations. It was also blessed with an ideal climate and rich deep soil for growing abundant crops. After 1784, it had a long period of prosperity and was second only to San Gabriel in the wealth of its possessions. It was famous for its fine weaving.

The church completed in 1825, the fifth church for the Santa Clara Mission, gave form to the replica built in 1929 that we see today.

After secularization, it continued as a church even though the wealth and possessions of the Mission were gone. In 1851, a need for English speaking Fathers for the new Americans, caused the Mission to be turned over to the Jesuits for a school. Four years later it became Santa Clara College, later the present university.

The church suffered a series of three fires, the last in 1926 totally destroying the building. The new church built in 1929 is the center of the University of Santa Clara campus. It also serves as a parish church and a college chapel.

San Buenaventura

(Ninth Mission, March 31, 1782)

What was to be the third Mission finally, after a 12 year delay, became the ninth Mission. It was the last Mission founded by Father Serra before his death. The long delay was caused by the discovery of San Francisco Bay that changed the priorities for settling California, and the uprising of the Yuma Indians in 1781. The Yuma revolt was against two Arizona style Missions, but it made the military in California fearful of an Indian uprising. Also, it was the result of a new government policy that made new Missions secondary to bringing Spanish settlers into Indian territory. Father Serra founded the Ventura Mission in the old style to Christianize the Indians, definitely against government policy.

The site was in a coastal area populated with about 20,000 Chumash Indians. The Chumash were among the most advanced tribes in California. They were skilled boat builders, excellent coastal seamen, fishermen, and the women knew how to weave reed baskets that were watertight.

The Mission prospered and was noted for its abundance of corps with a great variety of fruits and tropical plants. A reservoir and aqueduct system seven miles long was built to water the grain fields.

The first church burned in 1792, and was replaced in 1809 with the stone church that stands today. The large earthquake in 1812 caused much damage to the church. Almost four years of reconstruction was required to repair the building and strengthen it against future earthquakes. The large buttress at the front was added during this time.

After secularization in 1836, it served as a parish church, was sold, but was returned to the Catholic Church sixteen years later. An attempt to modernize it caused much damage to the original building. The beamed ceiling was covered over, the Indian artwork on the walls was whitewashed, and windows were enlarged and replaced with stained glass. In 1957, it was restored to its original form as much as possible. The City of Ventura has grown around the Church, but a recent plaza development in front of the building has added a sense of space for the historic structure.

Santa Bárbara

(Tenth Mission, December 4, 1786)

Santa Bárbara, like San Diego and Monterey, was named by Sebastian Vizcaino almost 186 years before the Mission was founded. The Franciscans have had continuous control over the Mission since its founding and its record are in an unbroken sequence. This is the only California Mission which has remained so.

The presidio was founded six years before the Mission, but the Governor said it had to be this way for security reasons. Once underway, the Mission grew very fast. The Indians were Chumash, a very advanced tribe. They planted and harvested crops that ranked sixth in Mission production. They were excellent craftsmen, excelled at building and the arts, including painting and music.

The elaborate water system was a great accomplishment. Water was flowed from a dam upstream from the Mission, collected in two large reservoirs, sent through filtered and settling tanks, and along elevated aqueducts to the kitchen, laundry, flour mill, and hospital, then finally to irrigate the fields and orchards. Parts of it are still used today as part of the municipal water system.

Its first permanent church, in 1789, was adobe with a tile roof. Within five years it was too small and a large church was built. It was destroyed by the earthquake in 1812. The present stone church was started shortly afterwards and dedicated in 1820. Only the left tower was completed at the time, the other being finished in 1833. It is the only Mission with twin towers.

Father Antonio Pipoll was responsible for building Mission Santa Bárbara. The Greco-Roman facade on the church was selected from a translation of Vitrivius' book on architecture written in 27 B.C. A copy was found in the Mission library.

The church continued in the hands of the Franciscans during secularization, but was damaged by a series of earthquakes. The most serious was in 1925 when one of the towers was destroyed and the second floor of the monastery severely damaged. The front of the church and towers were rebuilt to the original design in the restoration completed in 1927. Later cracks developed so, the present facade was completely rebuilt in reinforced concrete in 1950.

Mission Santa Bárbara is a true architectural gem of the Mission chain.

La Purísima Concepcion

(Eleventh Mission, December 8, 1787)

The original site of the Mission was in the present town of Lompoc. La Purisima was favored with fertile soil and friendly Indians but they needed to develop an elaborate irrigation system before the Mission started to prosper. By 1800, it had over 20,000 head of livestock and was third in agricultural production for all the Missions.

The first chapel and cluster of buildings were built in 1788 of wood poles and plastered with mud. In ten years this chapel was outgrown and a new church was started with adobe walls and a tile roof. This church served well a prosperous Mission until 1812.

Then catastrophe struck in the same earthquake of 1812 that damaged the large church at Santa Barbara. It leveled all the buildings of La Purisima, then broke a natural dam that flooded the ruins. Four months later, the Mission was re-established in its present location four miles north and east of its original site.

The new Mission had protection against earthquake damage with heavy buttressed stone walls. The buildings were laid out in straight lines for easier evacuation, the only Mission so arranged.

At the new site, it regained its earlier prosperity but further disasters were to come to the Mission in its final years. It suffered a severe drought, then fire destroyed some of the buildings, and finally the Indians rebelled against the soldiers in 1824. They occupied the buildings by force and held the Mission in siege for a month. A hundred soldiers came from Monterey before the Indians surrendered to the Fathers.

After secularization, the Mission disintegrated and what few Indians remained suffered a smallpox epidemic in 1844.

The Union Oil Company finally acquired some of the land and donated it so the Mission could be restored. The National Park Service directed the work of the Civilian Conservation Corps in rebuilding it from the ground up. A trip to the restored Mission, now a State Historical Monument, is almost like visiting the Mission in its golden years.

Santa Cruz

(Twelfth Mission, September 25, 1791)

A very pleasant setting where the San Lorenzo River flows into Monterey Bay gave great promise to the Mission's beginning. The land was covered with lush grass and berries. Wild game was plentiful. Forests of pine and redwood covered the mountains and the Indians were friendly. Progress was good at the new Mission, but was soon to go downhill rapidly. Santa Cruz never had more than 523 neophytes at its height.

In 1796, the Governor founded the third pueblo in California, named Branciforte, just across the river from the Mission. It was to be model city, but instead was populated with trouble makers from Mexico who founded the city rather than going to jail. The pueblo was such a degrading influence on the neophytes that over 200 left the Mission in the next two years. The Governor was petitioned to either move the pueblo or close the Mission. He decided to do neither.

Things were to get worse. Rain and high winds damaged the Mission buildings, then floods took their toll. The buildings were finally repaired to a usable condition.

In 1812, Father Andres Quintana was murdered by a group of renegade Indians in his sleep. In 1818, the rebel pirate Bouchard from Argentina was raiding the coast. He sacked Monterey. The Mission residents in Santa Cruz fled in fear that he might come in their direction. He didn't, but the people of Branciforte looted the mission worse than Bouchard and his men possibly could. Branciforte became a haven for adventurers and smugglers.

The Mission was secularized in 1834. An earthquake in 1840 destroyed the church so, by 1846, there was nothing left for Governor Pio Pico to sell. Another earthquake in 1857 tumbled the remaining walls. Mission Santa Cruz was no more.

Today a two thirds scale replica of the church stands not far from the Mission site. It was built in 1931 and generously donated to the Catholic church. Our drawing is of the replica.

Nuestra Señora de la Soledad

(Thirteenth Mission, October 9, 1791)

It has been said that la Soledad "was founded in solitude, and perished in neglect". The name was accidental because the natives seemed to call them selves soledad, the Spanish word for solitude. Thus the Mission was named after Our Lady of Solitude, another name for the Virgin Mary. It became a fitting name because life at the Mission was lonely and rather isolated. A total of 30 Fathers served at Soledad in the 44 years of its existence.

The lack of consistent leadership was more responsible for the Mission's reputation rather than its location. At times, the Mission managed to more than hold its own. It ranked in the middle in terms of agricultive production, which is not surprising with its location in the rich Salinas Valley. It was good cattle and sheep country in the hills. Irrigation water was available during the summer when it doesn't rain, through five miles of cemented ditch.

Several misfortunes added to Soledad's reputation. Starting in 1802, a serious epidemic killed many and drove off many more Indians. The Salinas River flooded the Mission in 1824, and even worse in 1828. The church collapsed in 1831. A store house was converted to a chapel that survived into secularization.

Father Sarria, the last Father at Soledad, kept the Mission going by himself from 1828 until he died in 1835, a year after secularization. Soledad was no longer an operating Mission.

Restoration was not started until 1954. Only one corner of wall remained intact at that time with several mounds of adobe. The chapel was built from the ground up first. More is being built as times goes on but it is still far from complete. Soledad is a parish church today. The drawing shows the rebuilt chapel.

San José

(Fourteenth Mission, June 11, 1797)

This Mission and the pueblo 15 miles south were envisioned as a base to control the Indians in the San Joaquin and Sacramento Valleys. Military expeditions were being sent to punish the troublesome tribes of the inland valleys, and this Mission was on the main route. The Indian tribes of the area were either indifferent or openly hostile to the Mission for the first few years.

However, the situation changed rapidly and San Jose became the most successful Mission in northern California. It ranked third behind Santa Clara and San Gabriel in the number converts with 6,673. It was third in livestock holdings and in total agriculture it was second only to San Gabriel.

Much of the success of the Mission is due to an extraordinary Father, Narciso Duran, who supervised it for 27 years. He excelled at everything he tried. He directed the elaborate Mission enterprises, planned military strategy against hostile Indians, constructed irrigation systems, and not the least of all, he wrote and taught music. His Indian orchestra became famous and played European instruments.

The Mission suffered the usual decline after secularization, but remained in use as a parish church. Slow deterioration was taking effect when an earthquake in 1868 brought the Mission to a violent end. It was the strongest quake in the recorded history of California. Only a small fragment of one wing of a quadrangle that once covered five acres remains today. The church in the drawing was built in 1809 and may have looked like this. A wooden structure was built in place of the adobe church but it was abandoned. Plans are now being made to rebuild the old Mission church on its original foundations.

San Juan Bautista

(Fifteenth Mission, June 24, 1797)

The Mission lies in a gentle, sunny valley separated from the Salinas Valley by the Gabilan mountains. It has been a parish church continuously since its founding, and its setting has changed little from a hundred years ago.

From the very beginning, it drew a large number of converts. Within six months they had constructed the Mission complex. By 1800, there were over 500 Indians living at the Mission. An earthquake caused considerable damage in October of that year. In rebuilding it, the Fathers enlarged the church. Even so, by 1803, a new larger church was started; the one that is there today. Father Arroyo de la Cuesta wanted a church for a 1,000 worshipers without the long, narrow nave. He convinced the builders that it should have a side aisle on each side of the nave, or basically a church with three naves side by side. When the building was finished in 1812, it was the largest and the only one of its kind.

By the time the church was finished, the Indian population was reduced by half through death and desertion. The church was too large so Cuesta walled in the two rows of arches that separated the naves thus forming a church with one nave.

For most its existence, the Mission was guided by Father Cuesta and Father Tapis, two most remarkable Fathers. Father Cuesta had a gift for language, as well as being architect, scholar, and musician. He mastered seven Indian dialects, could give his sermons in their own tongue, and could communicate with his charges in their language. Father Tapis was an accomplished musician and had a special talent for music. He used colored notes to identify the different vocal parts so the Indians could read music in choral singing.

The Mission had a flourishing trade with Yankee ships at Monterey, trading hides and tallow for machinery and other goods.

After secularization in 1834, the Indians gradually left, but the church was never without a priest.

A wooden steeple was added by Father Rubio in 1867.

The Mission is built on the San Andreas Fault, so the earthquake of 1906 did considerable damage. But Father Cuesta's walled in arches saved the main church.

The steeple was damaged by wind storm in 1915. The design was changed to a shorter version of a wooden steeple only to be modified again to a more Mission style stucco tower. Our drawing shows the Mission with its stucco tower. It was finally removed in 1949.

In 1976, extensive reconstruction returned the Mission to its original three naves, so once again it is California's largest Mission church. A new bell wall was added to complement the Mission style of architecture, not a restoration, but a whole new tower.

San Miguel Arcángel

(Sixteenth Mission, July 25, 1797)

Father Lasuen founded four Missions in four months. San Miguel was the third, located halfway between San Luis Obispo and San Antonio de Padua. The start of the Mission was very encouraging. A large crowd of Indians gathered for the dedication ceremonies. Fifteen children were baptized that day. However, there was a specific understanding that every effort would be made to attract the Tulare Indians from the San Joaquin valley. They were warlike tribes who resented any intrusion of the white man. Historical records indicate the Mission had very little success in this ambitious program.

The Mission was located in a fertile valley near the meeting place of two rivers, the Nacimiento and the Salinas. It quickly developed and became a thriving community.

In 1806, a serious fire destroyed a number of buildings and part of the church roof. The most immediate damage was to the stores of wool, cloth, leather goods and over 6,000 bushels of grain. With help from the other Missions, San Miguel soon recovered.

Work on the new church was started in 1816. Workmen had began making adobe bricks for this church almost six years earlier. Indians had cut and hauled large roof timbers from pine forests 40 miles away. The building was finished in 1818. Five years later, artist Esteban Munras taught and directed the Indians in fresco work that gives the interior a special radiance, that is still there today.

The arcade in front of the monastery is a unique touch indicating a creative builder with imagination and humor. The arches are not alike. Each is different from the one next to it, but a definite pattern exists. The first arch is a small semicircular one, followed by four larger ones, then a large elliptical arch to the centerline. The pattern is symmetrical about the centerline but all are very irregular.

San Miguel was one of the last Missions secularized. The last Franciscan left in 1840. In 1878, the property was returned to the Catholic Church. During the intervening years, the monastery was used as a series of stores. The church was unattended for long periods of time and it is surprising that the interior remains in its original condition. The Franciscans returned to the Mission in 1928. Today it is a parish church and maintained in a manner to express its rich history.

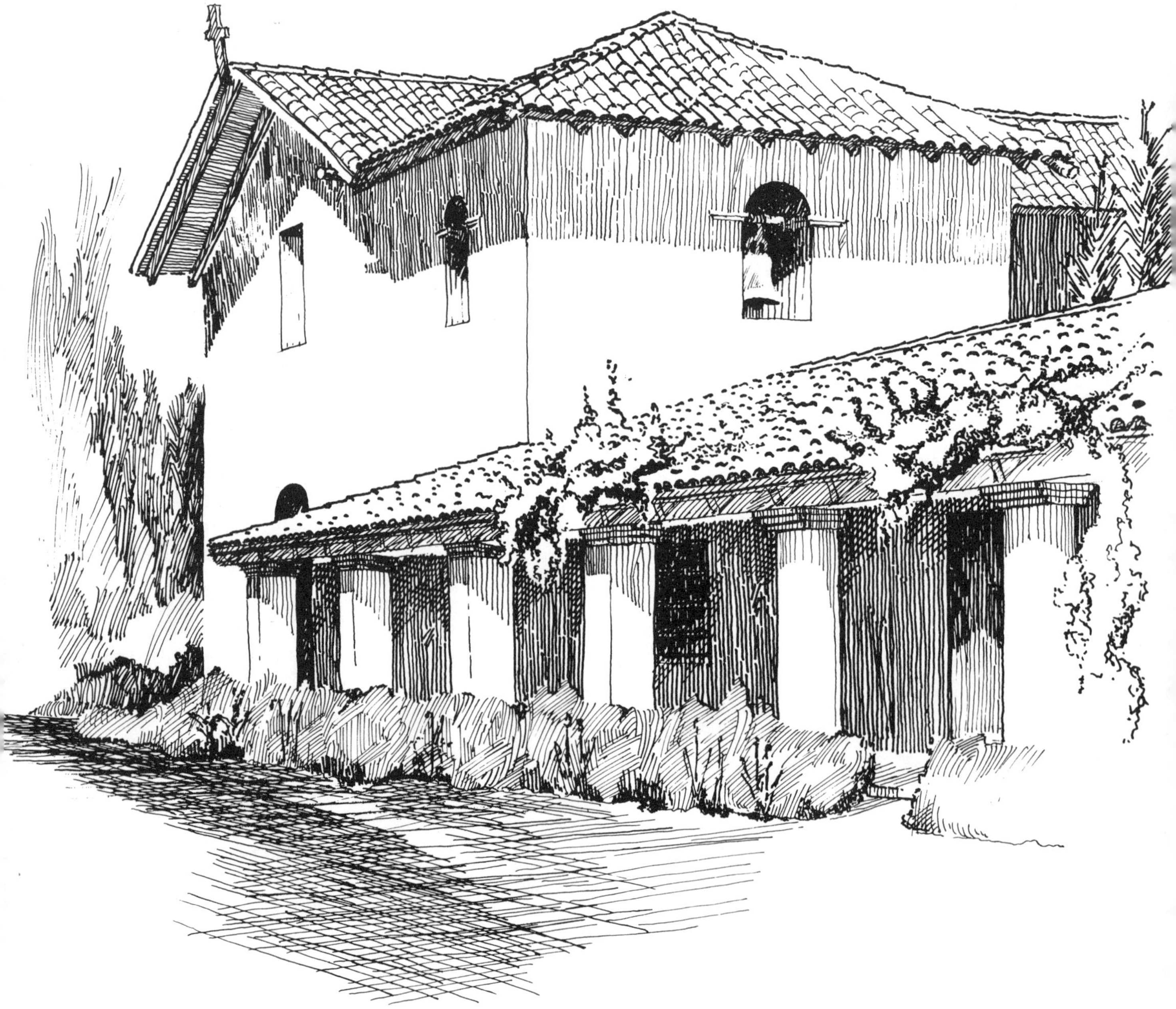

San Fernando Rey de España

(Seventeenth Mission, September 8, 1797)

San Fernando was the fourth Mission founded by Father Lasuen in a four months period in 1797. They were all part of the inland chain of Missions located to maintain a day's travel distance between Missions. As with the other inland Missions, success was almost immediate. Many Indians attended the dedication and ten children were baptised that day. Within two months a small church was completed and forty neophytes were living at the Mission.

The founding of the Mission was different in several respects. The site for the buildings was on a private rancho owned by Don Francisco Reyes, a Spanish settler. There seems to be some question whether he received the land as a grant from the King or just settled on it. But he obviously gave it up gracefully for the Mission.

The Mission then was less than a day's travel from the well established and rapidly growing peublo of Los Angeles. The Mission became the most popular place to stop for travelers from Los Angeles on El Camino Real. Overnight guests were always welcome at the Mission. The need for hospice space resulted in construction of the famous "long building." After thirteen years it was to reach 243 feet in length. It is today the largest original structure remaining in the Mission chain and the largest adobe building in California. The long two-story building proved valuable to subsequent owners after secularizaiton. It remained intact and well maintained. The church wasn't so lucky. The roof tiles were sold and the walls allowed to erode away.

Gold was discovered on an outer rancho of the Mission in 1843, five years before the great California gold discovery. A mini-rush occurred after this discovery but the scale of the gold find did not excite too many people.

San Fernando was involved in military operations on several occasions. It was the military head-quarters for California governors from 1833 until 1846, and John C. Fremont made it his headquarters after he captured it in 1847.

In 1896, The Landmark Club started a campaign to restore the buildings. Restoration has been more or less continuous ever since. The earthquake of 1971 caused considerable damage.

San Luis Rey de Francia

(Eighteenth Mission, June 13, 1798)

The timing was ideal for the founding of this Mission. Although a very late Mission, it became one of the most successful. The Indians were almost anxious to become part of this new enterprise, and could see the definite economic advantages in their lives.

One of the important reasons for the success or failure of any Mission was the Father-in-charge. For San Luis Rey, this talented man was Father Antonio Peyri who directed its fortunes from the founding for the next thirty-three years. The organizing genius of Father Peyri developed an endless number of thriving industries. The extent of its land holdings, the size of its herds of sheep, cattle, and horses, and even the size of the Indian village was greater than that of any other Mission.

Father Peyri proved to be an able architect as well. He drew the plans and supervised construction of a vast array of buildings and other construction projects such as an intricate aqueduct system, large open-air laundry and bath facilities with pools of charcoal-filtered water, and extensive gardens.

The large church that exists today was started in 1811 and finished in 1815 — remarkable in itself when we realize the great stone church at San Juan Capistrano was destroyed by an earthquake in 1812. The church is the most sophisticated architecturally and one of the most interesting of all the Missions. The plan is in the form of a cross (cruciform) similar to the ruined church at San Juan Capistrano, the only other so constructed. It has an elaborate octagonal baptistry roofed with a dome, and another dome over the cross. Later a raised lantern with windows for light was built on top of this dome. The title "King of the Missions" is in part due to the church construction.

Father Peyri left the Mission in 1832 because of pressure from the new Mexican government and the approach of secularization. What was left was sold in 1846. President Lincoln signed the decree returning the Missions to the church in 1861, but by then the desolation was almost complete.

Franciscan Fathers from Mexico asked for and received permission to establish a seminary in 1893 at the Mission. Restoration continued off and on from then until 1950 when it was substantially complete. The church remains now very much as it was during its glory days.

Santa Inés

(Nineteenth Mission, September 17, 1804)

The last of the southern Missions and nineteenth over all, was founded by Father Estevan Topis to serve the numerous Indians inland, across the mountains from Santa Barbara. The Indians were aware of the missionary effort so over 200 were present when the blessing was bestowed. Twenty children were baptized.

Santa Ines had all of the possibilities of becoming an outstanding Mission. Even though it was moderately successful, it never lived up to its great potential. Its pleasant setting in the beautiful valley of the Santa Ines River gave no indication of the troubles that would keep it from that potential.

The strong earthquake of 1812 destroyed many of the numerous building constructed at the Mission and damaged the church to the extent that five years of reconstruction were required before it was rededicated. During that time a new long building was hastily built to be used as a church, then later used as a granary when it was no longer needed for religious services.

Starting in 1810, the Missions had to support the military forces stationed to guard them. After Mexico gained her independence in 1821, the cost to support the soldiers was increased. Indians resented doing so much for the idle soldiers and taking abuse from them also. In 1824, after a soldier beat a neophyte for a minor infraction, open revolt resulted in an attack by the Indians on the Mission. They burned some of the buildings but when the church started to burn, the Indians paused long enough to help put the fire out. Even though the revolt was not against the Fathers, Indian relations were never the same again.

In 1836, Santa Inés was shared with the civil administration, a first step to secularization. The decline was rapid but the Mission was saved from complete ruin by an agreement between the Governor and the Bishop to open a college. Opened in 1844, it became the first college in California. The College of Our Lady of Refuge. It was later moved and remained open only until 1881.

The first real effort to restore the Mission was in 1904 by the parish priest, Father Alexander Buckler. In 1924, the Capuchin Franciscans took over. Major reconstruction work was done in 1947 and 1953.

San Rafael Arcángel

(Twentieth Mission, December 14, 1817)

San Rafael Mission was founded as a branch of Mission Dolores for one primary reason, and a secondary reason acceptable to the civil authorities. The weather at Mission Dolores, especially in the summer, was damp, foggy and cold. The Indians were not able to tolerate this climate. Hundreds had died and many more were chronically ill. Just north across the bay, San Rafael was protected by the mountain from the wind and fog offering a warmer, dry climate for the sick neophytes. It was founded as a sanitarium for the sick from Mission Dolores, and named after the Archangel Raphael, whose name means "God's healing power".

The secondary reason was the Russians, who had established a fur trading outpost at Ft. Ross in 1812. The Spanish didn't want them to expand further south into this territory.

Father Luis Gil y Toboado from La Purísima Mission was asked to be an advisor on establishing the sanitarium, being the only Father in California with some medical training. Father Gil volunteered to run the Mission branch, with immediate success. Before long, the sick from other Missions were also being sent to San Rafael. It not only was a healing place for the sick, but the Mission prospered and became self-sufficient.

The buildings were not complicated or imposing. They consisted of a church with a long wing for the Father's quarters, workshops, storerooms, and hospital wards. It is supposed the church had a star window like, but smaller than Carmel, as its only decoration. Even this is not known for certain. It was raised to the status of a full Mission in 1823.

San Rafael was the first Mission secularized. General Vallejo took over the lands and livestock to protect them from improper use, and for later distribution to the Indians. Vallejo had much land as a probable result of this. The Mission was abandoned in 1855. By 1861 the building was sold to a carpenter who demolished the remains to salvage the large handhewn beams.

In 1949 a replica of the Mission was built with a donation from the Hearst Foundation. The replica faces the mountains, the original faced the bay. This drawing is of the replica.

San Francisco de Solano

(Twenty-first Mission, July 4, 1823)

Still fearful that the Russians might move farther south, the Spanish authorities planned a series of settlements to extend north almost to Ft. Ross. Missions were to be established at Sonoma, Santa Rosa, and Napa with a presidio at Bodega Bay.

Into this plan came a young Father stationed at Mission Dolores, Father Jose Altimira. Recently arrived in California from Spain, Father Altimira was full of missionary zeal and anxious to convert the Indians. He developed an ambitious scheme to close the Missions at Dolores and San Rafael, with the idea of combining all of their assets into one large, prosperous Mission farther north. Without the knowledge or approval of Father President Senan, Father Altimira received approval from the Governor and founded the Mission at Sonoma. When the Church authorities learned of the scheme, they rebuked both the Governor and Father Altimira. A compromise was finally reached to let the Mission at Sonoma remain as San Francisco Solano, but Mission Dolores and San Rafael would also continue.

Father Altimira lacked leadership abilities and in about two years, the Indians revolted against his harsh treatment and forced him to flee to San Rafael.

A large adobe church was completed in 1833, but by then the winds of change were too much to allow development as a typical Mission. General Vallejo took over the Mission after secularization as chief administrator in 1835.

Vallejo is responsible for building the present chapel in 1840 because decay of the large church was so rapid.

The Russians withdrew from Ft. Ross in 1841. The increasing number of Americans were afraid Mexico wanted them out of California, so on June 14, 1846 some of the Americans took over Sonoma and made Vallejo a prisoner. They flew a crude flag with a grizzly bear and star, declaring California an independent republic. The republic lasted 23 days before Commodore Sloat raised the American flag in Monterey.

Vallejo's chapel that stands today has been restored a number of times. The Landmarks League in 1903 bought the ruins, but the 1906 earthquake damaged the remains so work was very slow. The state acquired the building in 1926, restored it again in 1944, and it is now a State Historical Monument.

View Spanish California Today

Often parents and/or community members will be a big help in sharing experiences, craft pieces, recipes, to say nothing of themselves.

Walking field trips to Mexican stores of all kinds; supermercados will be a big help.

If you take a Mission trip, plan what to look for with the children.

There is hardly a book on Missions that doesn't have at least one artifact in the contents (illustration) and can be shown through opaque or overhead projectors.

Be sure to check your Instructional Media Center for more films, film strips, slides, and other resources they may have.

Remember that the ultimate goal here is to help build for boys and girls understandings to their fullest of the California Missions, as a part of history and as they influence our lives today.

Environmental Board

1. Arrange children in groups of five or six. Each group will have one board (cardboard or wood, about the size of two desk tops)
2. Using any materials available to them and appropriate to the task, children will build an environment representing a piece of California land. It may be two or three dimensional. Teacher should begin by listing some elements that all boards should have, such as:
   — a water source
   — a wooded area
   — a grassy area
   — hills
   Let them represent this in any way they choose. They could use paint, colored paper, clay, pipe cleaners, materials some kids have for building model train outfits. Some may want to include animal figures (this should be okay if historically and geographically accurate — deer, yes, tigers no.).

3. Prepare ditto to be duplicated on tagboard, with small drawn figures of people, such as missionaries, soldiers, settlers, and Indians. You might wish to make two dittos with the first, Indians, then settlers.
4. After preparation of "environment" give each group a card of people. Let them cut the figures apart and then show answers to specific questions. For Indians, it might be . . . . How would they provide shelter? How would they find food in this area? How would they protect themselves from dangers? For settlers, it might be . . . . How would a group of missionaries use this area? Where would they build houses? Where would they grow crops? Where could settlements be built for trading? Later, for both groups, questions, such as: How would Indians and settlers live together in this area?

As learning goes on, models of Missions or of settlements could be added to the boards.

How Hides Were Prepared for Shipment

The hide of the cattle was probably the most important part of the animal to the ranchero. The hides were used for many things in early California. Hides and also tallow were used almost like money in trading on the ships that came, bringing clothes and many other fine things desired by the people of California.

When the hide was taken from the animal it was spread out and staked to dry. They were then put through a process called curing. This made them easier to handle and helped to keep them from spoiling. They were soaked in a very salty water solution for many hours and then spread out to dry. They were then stretched on the ground and were left to dry. Next they were powdered with salt. When the hides were ready, men folded them in half with the hair on the outside.

Papier Maché Made Easy

The easiest way of making papier maché objects is to apply glued strips of newspapers, paper towels, craft paper — whatever paper you have on hand — to a base. Strips that have been torn rather than cut have a rough edge and will mesh together for a smoother surface. If you are applying several layers of strips, it is wise to use a different color or type of of paper for each layer. You can alternate between white and colored newspaper or paper toweling, using white facial tissue for the final cover. Use mash for giving texture.

Bases that can be used:
- boxes for Mission making
- tuna cans with paper cylinders for candle holders
- t.v. dinner trays can be molded for masks

Paper Mash. Paper mash, or pulp, is made by soaking or cooking paper in water and combining with starch to form a malleable substance. It can be molded over a base or by itself, and used to add texture or to build up specific areas. There are several commercial mixes available for making "instant" paper mash. These mixtures are easy to work with and readily available at hobby or craft stores also.

Sheet Papier-Maché. Stack two sheets of white paper towel or facial tissue on top of four sheets of newspaper. Draw the shape you want on the top sheet in crayon or pencil. Cut this shape out of the stack of papers. Brush or sponge a heavy coat of liquid starch over each layer of the cut-out shape. Press the layers together firmly. Sculpture by bending, pleating, or folding. Large pieces must be put over a box, can, or bottle to hold the shape while drying. Let sculpture dry for 24 to 36 hours.

Mission Fruits and Vegetables

Using the same technique as described in making Maracas, make papier maché fruits and vegetables. Put strip mache over vaselined fruits and let dry. Cut and remove fruit or vegetable. Paint and shellac. Prepare a Mission fruit basket.

A Sombrero

You can use a styrene hat from a pizza parlor, an old hat, or a party hat from a variety store as a base to make this colorful Mexican sombrero. Begin by attaching a wide circle of heavy cardboard to the brim with rubber cement and tape. Then crumple newspaper and tape to the hat top for a rounder and fuller shape. Drape a large sheet of newspaper over the built-up crown and secure with string or a rubber band. Cover the hat *(inside and out)* with five layers of newspaper strips dipped in liquid starch. Add a final layer of paper towel strips. Set aside to dry. Paint with bright red acrylics, adding yellow trim; for a shiny surface cover with a coat of shellac. Glue on balled fringe and a ribbon hatband.

Book Binding

Punch three matching holes in the pages and in the front and back covers of the book. With a straight edge or rule, fold and crease the front cover about two inches from its left end to make a hinge. Stack the pages and covers together so that the holes align. Thread the holes with ribbon, yarn, or string and tie the book together.

Wire Weaving with Bobby Pin Shuttle

Use a wire cutter, cut chicken wire or hardware cloth into the desired shape. Cover all the cut ends of the wire with masking tape. Weave designs and patterns on the wire with yarn, ribbon, and string of all sorts of colors, textures, and thicknesses. Tie one end of the material to the wire. Pierce the other end with a bobby pin and pull it through to the closed end of the pin. Weave over and under the wires — one, two, three, or more at a time. When you are finished with any one kind of material, tie to the wire frame. Then tie the new piece to the frame, poke in the bobby pin, and continue weaving. The protective masking tape can be removed, or replaced with cloth tape, when the piece is finished. You'll get a true weaving feeling and can make your own Mission Indian hanging or table mats. Try dyeing your own yarns with vegetable dyes.

Getting in Touch

Instead of having penpals really far away, find a new friend or a class in California with whom to correspond. If you live near a Mission, find a class in the mountains or in the desert; if you live far away from the Missions you might want to find some children near a Mission. This will broaden the the scope of understanding of the state. Share the Spanish names of places with your pen class. What questions might you ask?

Teachers and parents: Check state school directories for public or private school addresses.

From CSAA get maps and hunt for Spanish names.

Dear Mom, Dad, Boys, Girls, and Teachers:

At some time during the fourth grade you will probably want to write to a Mission. Check the address and status of your special Mission and enclose a stamped, self-addressed envelope for easy answering.

George Kuska
Barbara Linse

Group Work—Murals/Movies

WHAT TO HAVE:

A class full of children to divide into groups of four to six for work on various phases of a broader topic, through diorama, movies or friezes.

HOW TO DIVIDE:

1. Choose as many group leaders as you will have topics or groups. Let them select their children.
2. Cut up little pieces of paper. Write numbers on them, i.e., have five #1s, etc.
3. Teacher select own groups.

HOW TO MAKE USE:

Direct into film, work, puppet shows, murals, etc.

GROUP WORK — PARCHMENT PAPER

Make Parchment Paper for writing or printing important legal documents as you see the need to reproduce them in your classroom, such as the Decree of Secularization.

Materials:

— one sheet of waxpaper
— facial tissue
— liquid starch or white glue

Cover the waxpaper with liquid starch or diluted white glue. Cover, overlapping, as needed, with full sheets of facial tissue. Pat dry. When completely dry, print or write documents on tissue side with felt pen.

Mission Music

Music was a part of Mission life. Both the Indian groups and the Spanish had used chants and singing for work, worship and pleasure. The Mission Bells were important and pealed far and wide to bring workers out of the fields to meal or worship.

Simple rhythm instruments were made and used to give a beat to renditions. *Maracas*, as shown, were coming, as were rubbing gutty sticks together for what are called *matracas*.

As you visit and correspond with the people of the Missions ask them for Mission music hints.

MATRACAS *(Music & Rhythm)*

Noise or rhythm instruments were fashioned in various manners. Ways of making noise or rhythm:
1. Hit 2 sticks together
2. Put seeds in large shells and shake
3. Tie shells or acorns or little pine cones together and shake
4. With a stick give a large cone "a rubdown" and it will whiz for you.

How else could Indians and Padres make beautiful music together? Think of instruments and be your own factory.

MUSIC MARACAS OR NOISEMAKERS

By using an orange as a base, you can make a Mexican *maraca* or a "baby rattle." You will also need two ½-inch dowels and a package of dried, edible beans.

First, cover the orange with petroleum jelly for easy removal later on. Then apply six layers of paper towel strips dipped in starch. *(or flour and water mixture)* Be careful not to use too much or the surface will not dry rapidly enough and the orange may spoil. For a smooth surface, add a final layer of paper towel strips. Place on waxed paper and allow to dry for at least 48 hours, turning the covered orange two or three times during this period to permit even drying. Then draw a line around the center for a cutting guide. Using a sharp knife, cut the dried papier maché into two halves and remove the orange. Tape the two halves together and cover the joint with two layers of paper towel squares. Then cover the entire surface with a layer of paper towel strips. Allow to dry. To add the handle, use scissors or a craft knife and cut a hole ½-inch in diameter in the *maraca*. Drop in several beans to make the rattling sound. Put a drop of white glue on the end of a ½-inch dowel; then push the dowel into the hole until it touches the other side. To hold it in place, drive a nail through the surface into the top of the dowel. To strengthen the *maraca*, coat it with shellac. When it is dry, use acrylics to paint on a Mission design. Remember to use non-toxic paints for a baby's rattle.

A COLORED-NOTE SONG BOOK

Learn to sing in parts as the neophytes did at Mission Santa Barbara — the colored-note way.

For our 3-part singing:
    light grey notes — melody
    dark grey notes — lower voices
    black notes — lowest voices

We can write chants telling of many things that went on at the Missions. Here's an easy-to-use sample of a simple but significant poem set to 3-part singing:

Get up now	tend the plow
Horse in hand	round the bend
Morning light	birds in flight
Time to dine	get in line

A	SO	LA	SO	SO	SO	SO
	MI	FA	MI	MI	RE	MI
	DO	DO	DO	DO	TI	DO
	Get	*up*	*now*	*tend*	*the*	*plow*

B	SO	SO	SO	SO	LA	SO
	MI	RE	MI	MI	FA	MI
	DO	TI	DO	DO	DO	DO
	Horse	*in*	*hand*	*round*	*the*	*bend*

C	SO	SO	LA	SO	LA	SO
	MI	RE	MI	MI	FA	MI
	DO	DO	DO	DO	DO	DO
	Morn – ing		*light*	*birds*	*in*	*flight*

D	SO	SO	LA	SO	SO	SO
	MI	MI	FA	RE	RE	MI
	DO	DO	DO	TI	TI	DO
	Time	*to*	*dine*	*get*	*in*	*line*

Mission Life Word Search

You will find among these letters 30 words related to people and things about the Missions.

The words are found by reading up, down, forward, backward and even diagonally. Enclose each word by drawing lines around it.

Parents and teachers: challenge yourselves and your youngsters by hiding the key for a spell.

acorn	bellows	corn	game	olla	San Diego
adobe	brick	dance	hides	Pacific	Serra
baja	burro	el camino	horses	padre	Solano
baskets	caballo	farm	Indian	pomo	tallow
bell	carreta	fiesta	Mission	roots	vaca

This puzzle was created by "Aunt" Margaret Johnson.

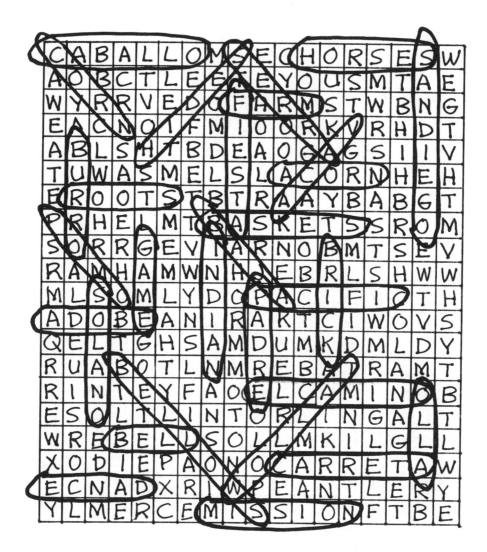

HERE IS THE SOLUTION! HOW DID YOU DO?

Mission Crafts and Skills

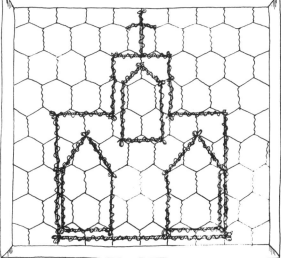

MISSION WEAVING

Large looms were used for cloth making in increasing numbers throughout the years. To give the feeling of weaving a pattern use chicken wire or hardware cloth is suggested as step 1. Box looms, waist looms, and card looms are among other simple homemade looms you might want to use in your home or classroom.

Materials — Wire
— Yarn
— Safety pins
— Bobby pins

MISSION MODELS have been made of everything from graham crackers to carved styrafoam *(carved gently with a sharp knife)*. Little adobe bricks are certainly the most authentic. Corrugated cardboard and lasagne noodles are among the materials which can be used to make ripply roofs.

Materials — See the choices.

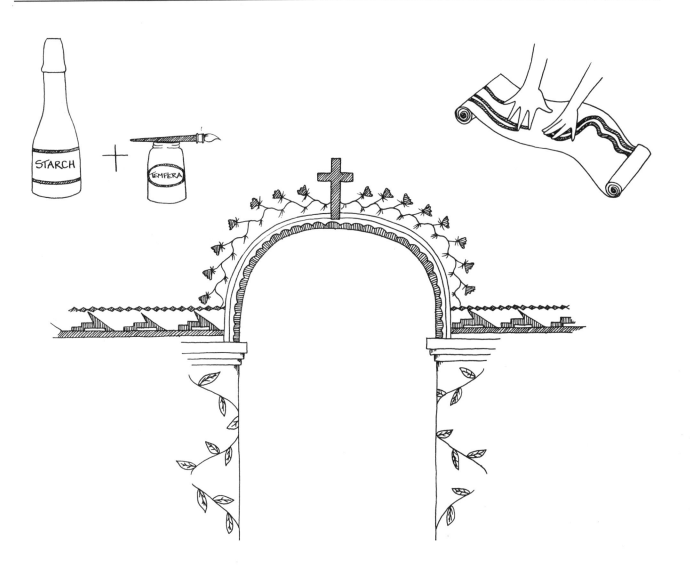

MISSION WALL FRIEZE OR DECORATION

Many of the Missions had simple patterns painted on the walls.

Many of the Missions had geometric or natural patterns painted on their walls.

How to Do It

Create a dozen zig zags and California poppies or oak leaves and acorns by repeating the patterns over and over with tempera and a brush on manila paper, a wall or shelf paper. Make geometric designs with starch and tempera and applying with fingers on shelf or butcher paper.

Materials — Hands or brushes.
          — Shelf paper
          — Paint and starch to equal finger paint

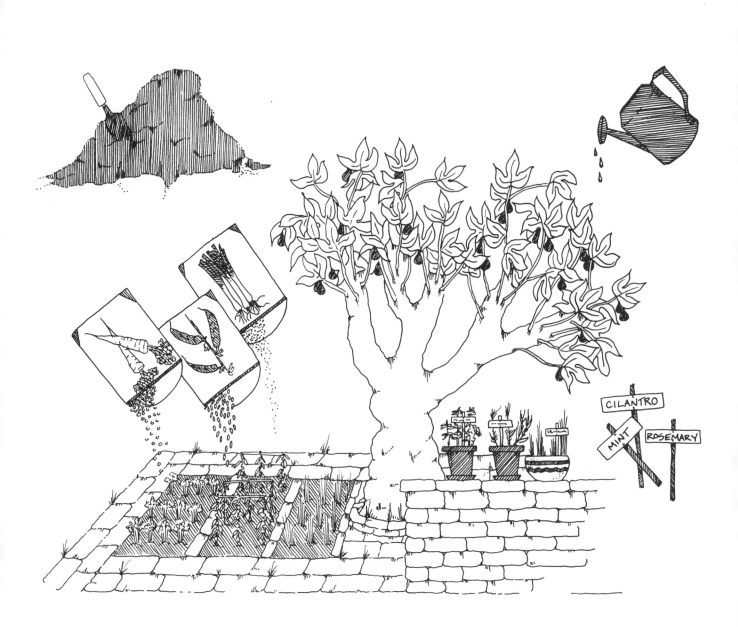

PLANT A MISSION GARDEN

Check your list of Mission produce for authenticity.
If you haven't space outside, flower pots inside
are fine.

WIRE COAT HANGER BRANDS

What are brands? With the coming of cattle to California and the separation into herds came the need to distinguish between different owners. Pieces of iron were forged into shapes peculiar to each ranch and Mission. This method of identification is used today. The iron is put in hot coals then onto the steer's flank.

Make your own shape or copy some you find here or in a library Mission or rancho book. Unwind the coat hanger; bend it into shape; and hang it up. Don't dump it in the coals!

Materials — Wire hanger

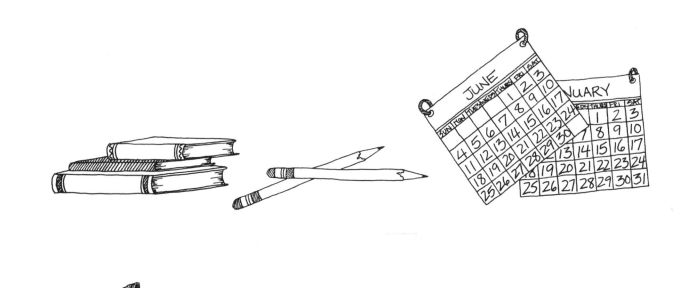

JOURNAL LOG AND DIARY KEEPING are useful experiences. The content can come from reading, from movies, individual projects or can be your own imagination of what some of these early experiences might have been.

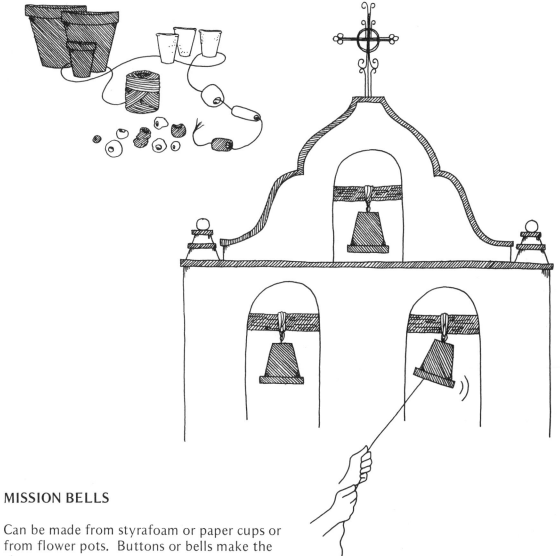

MISSION BELLS

Can be made from styrafoam or paper cups or
from flower pots. Buttons or bells make the
clappers.

Materials — Flower pots
            — Seeds or bells
            — Cups
            — String

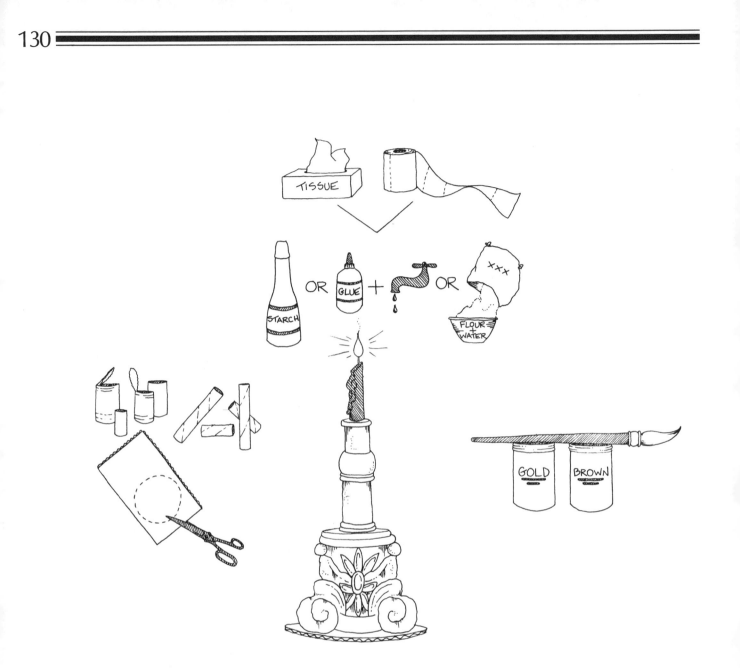

PAPIER MACHÉ MISSION CANDLE HOLDERS

Use cardboard circles, tubes, metal cans, spools and papier maché from toilet tissue and flour and water paste. Apply and mold with hands or sticks. Dry and paint.

Materials — Cardboard - flat or cylinders
— Scissors
— Mache
— Paint

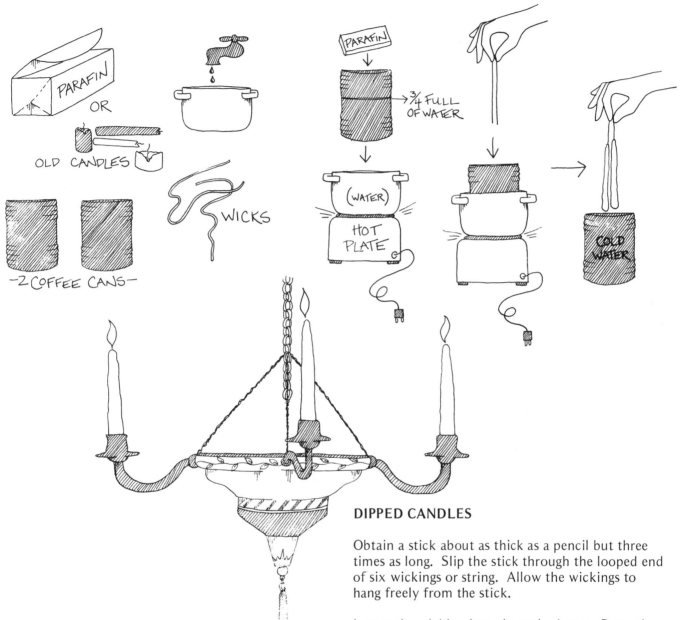

PARAFIN

OR

OLD CANDLES

-2 COFFEE CANS-

WICKS

PARAFIN → ¾ FULL OF WATER

(WATER) HOT PLATE

COLD WATER

DIPPED CANDLES

Obtain a stick about as thick as a pencil but three times as long. Slip the stick through the looped end of six wickings or string. Allow the wickings to hang freely from the stick.

Lower the wicking into the melted wax. Draw the wicking out and allow the wax to harden. Repeat the process until you have a candle of the proper size.

If more than one candle rod is used, you can dip one set of wickings while the wax is hardening on the others. Use the safe and tidy methods in the pictures.

Materials — Paraffin or old candles
— Hot plate or stove
— Cans
— Water
— Wicking or thread

MAPS

Relief Maps

Relief maps may be made by using papier maché or a salt and flour mixture, as shown in the illustration.

Acetate-Overlay Map

Use crayons or marking pens on a clear piece of acetate to add detail; overlay on your basic map.

PAST

ADOBE CLAY + SAND +

ADOBE BRICK MAKING

Use the materials, as shown, with 3 parts clay to 1 part sand and enough water to make a workable substance. Large wooden forms are used for big bricks. Big or little match boxes make fine molds depending on the projected size of your Mission.

Materials — Adobe clay
— Sand
— Water
— Straw for binding molds

PRESENT

POWDERED TERRA COTTA CLAY + SAND +

STORE IN PLASTIC

Matches
MATCHES
MATCHES

PLANNING A CULMINATION INVITATION

Haul of Records

Time Line for Spanish California

Pre-Columbian until Columbus discovered the Americas

The California Indians lived in California from who knows when until 1769, undisturbed.

1492 — Columbus discovered America
1512 — Cortez came to Mexico
1521 — Magellan to Manilla. The trading with the Manilla galleons began.
1533 — Cortez to Baja California
1542 — Cabrillo explored the coasts of Baja and Alta California
1596 — Viscaino sailed up the coast of Baja California
1602 — Viscaino to Alta California

1615 — Captain Juan de Iturbi explored the Baja Peninsula
1683 — Father Kino and the Jesuits explored Baja Peninsula for future missioning
1697 — First Baja Mission founded by the Jesuits
1768 — The Franciscans came and the Jesuits left Baja
1769 — The Franciscans left Baja and went to Alta California and established Mission San Diego de Alcala
1769 — 1824 — Twenty-one Missions established in Alta California
1834 — Secularization

Baja California Missions

Religious Order	Mission	Founding Date	Present Condition
Jesuit	Loreto	1697	Stone - rebuilt
Jesuit	San Javier	1699	Stone - good
Jesuit	Ligui	1705	Tile floor
Jesuit	Mulege	1705	Stone
Jesuit	Comondu	1708	Stone ruins
Jesuit	La Purisima	1719	Stone ruins
Jesuit	La Paz	1720	All gone
Jesuit	Guadalupe (Sur)	1720	Stone foundation
Jesuit	Dolores	1721	Adobe ruins
Jesuit	Santiago	1724	All gone
Jesuit	San Ignacio	1728	Stone
Jesuit	San Jose del Cabo	1730	All gone
Jesuit	San Miguel (Sur)	1730	All gone
Jesuit	Todos Santos	1734	Rebuilt - Adobe
Jesuit	San Luis Gonzaga	1737	Stone
Jesuit	La Pasion	1737	Stone ruins
Jesuit	Santa Gertrudis	1752	Stone
Jesuit	San Borja	1762	Stone
Jesuit	Calamajue	1766	Adobe ruins
Jesuit	Santa Maria	1767	Adobe ruins
Franciscan	San Fernando	1769	In ruins - Adobe as shown
Dominican	El Rosario	1774	Adobe ruins
Dominican	Santo Domingo	1775	Adobe ruins
Dominican	San Vicente	1780	Adobe ruins
Dominican	San Miguel de la Frontera	1787	Adobe ruins
Dominican	Santo Tomas	1791	Adobe ruins
Dominican	San Pedro Martir	1794	Stone foundation
Dominican	Santa Catalina	1797	Adobe ruins
Dominican	Descanso	1814	All gone
Dominican	Guadalupe (Notre)	1834	All gone

Mission Founding Dates

Mission	Namesake	Founding Date
San Diego de Alcalá	Saint Didacus of Alcala	Jul. 16, 1769
San Carlos Borromeo de Carmelo	Saint Charles Borromeo of Carmel	Jun. 3, 1770
San Antonio de Padua	St. Anthony of Padua	Jul. 14, 1771
San Gabriel Arcángel	St. Gabriel the Archangel	Sep. 8, 1771
San Luis Obispo de Tolosa	St. Louis of Tolosa	Sep. 1, 1772
San Juan de Capistrano	St. Juan of Capistrano	Nov. 1, 1776
San Francisco de Asís *(often known as Mission Dolores)*	St. Francis de Asis	Jun. 29, 1776
Santa Clara de Asís	St. Clara of Asis	Jan. 12, 1777
San Buenaventura	St. Good Fortune	Mar. 31, 1782
Santa Barbara	St. Barbara	Dec. 4, 1786
La Purísima Concepcion	The Pure Conception	Dec. 8, 1787
Santa Cruz	St. Cross	Aug. 28, 1791
Nuestra Señora de la Soledad	Our Lady of Loneliness	Oct. 9, 1791
San Jose *(please pronounce Hosay)*	St. Joseph	Jun. 11, 1797
San Juan Bautista	St. John the Baptist	Jun. 24, 1797
San Miguel Arcángel	St. Michael the Archangel	Jul. 25, 1797
San Fernando Rey de España	St. Ferdinand, King of Spain	Sep. 8, 1797
San Luis Rey de Francia	St. Louis, King of France	Jun. 13, 1798
Santa Inés	St. Inez	Sep. 17, 1804
San Rafael Arcángel	St. Rafael the Archangel	Dec. 14, 1811
San Francisco Solano	St. Francis of Solano	Jul. 4, 1823

Indian Games

THE INDIAN NUT-DICE GAME

Though this is mostly a woman's game among the Indians, it was widespread.

Materials:

— walnut shells, emptied and used as dice
— 200 sticks or teeny bones used as counters
— a basket to keep the materials in order

It's how you play the game that counts. Shake the shells in your hands and toss into a basket. Three up and three down gives the tosser 2 points; all tossed on one side gets 3 points. You get to take a stick or a bone for every point you make. Game is over when the sticks or bones are used up.

HAND OR GRASS GAME

Played by both men and women *(separate games)*

Materials:	2 pair of bones — one pair marked with sinew bands, other pair unmarked.
Players:	Two players on each of two teams
Rule:	Each person on one team has a pair of bones hidden in his hands
Scoring:	Each member of the guessing team guesses which hand the marked bone is in.

Neither guess is correct — boneholders get 2 points
Both guesses are correct — guessers get 2 points
One guess right — guessers get one point, and incorrectly guessed boneholder takes another turn at hiding bones.

STICK GAME

Predominantly played by men

Materials:	44 sticks
Object:	Correctly guess the remainder when the random number of sticks is divided into groups of four, i.e., 1, 2, 3, 4
Scoring:	Number guessed correctly — guesser wins the sticks
	Number guessed incorrectly — guesser lost bet (most probably given to him at 4-to-1 odds)

Products and Processes Brought to California by Spain

RANCHING AND ANIMAL HUSBANDRY:

Horses — Horsemanship, roundup, branding, lariat, rodeo, barbeque, stirrups, spurs, chaps, sombrero, corral

Cattle and Oxen — Meat, hides, tallow, candles

Burros and Mules — Riding, working, trading, hauling

Sheep — Mutton, wool, carding, spinning, weaving, sewing

Goats — Meat, milk, hair. Leaders for sheep

Chickens — Meat, eggs, feathers. Cockfights

AGRICULTURE AND HORTICULTURE

Introduction of grains — wheat, rye, oats, barley, rice *(and maize from Mexico).* Need for granaries, mills, millstones. Irrigation, cultivation, harvest. Calendar.

Alfalfa and hay crops — Forage for livestock. Tools for cutting, storage.

Vegetable gardens — Carrots, onions, garlic, lettuce, tomatoes, chiles, squash, peas, potatoes, yams.

Herb gardens — Peppercorn, marjoram, oregano.

Vineyards — Grapes, arbors, wineries, brandy distillation, Table grapes.

Olive orchards — Olive oil, presses *(rotary and upright),* storage jars.

Citrus — Oranges and lemons.

Fruit and nut orchards — Apple, peach, pear, fig, almond, walnut.

Irrigation — Ditches, reservoirs, aqueducts, fountains, techniques for raising water, wells.

The plow — Animal and human traction.

Transport of crops — Carretas, roads.

MARITIME ACTIVITIES

Fishing — Clams, crabs, salmon and ocean fish. Boats. Some European techniques and tools.

Sea otter. — Skins. Trade item. Techniques of harpooning. Aleuts imported by Russians and Yankees with their canoes.

Whaling — Oil, tusks.

Port facilities — Hide houses, docks, lighters.

Defenses — lighthouses.

Contact with Sandwich Islands*(Hawaii),* Mexico, China, Boston, England.

MISSION AND TOWN-BUILDING by:

Colonists: Padres and others
Retired soldiers
Christianized Indians
Foreigners

Make Mission Days Live

This activity is designed to inspire creativity and questions like *"How would I have done. . . .if I were there?"* Each group of children is supplied with an array of natural materials; for example, tules, bark, acorns, bones, black walnuts, soapstone, pictures of Mission pieces, etc.; and is asked to respond to a particular pressing problems. Response to such a problem helps each child realize the ingeniousness of the California Indians and early settlers' response to the same real life situations. "Pressing Problems" used successfully include: design a Mission, design a game, tell a legend, make a musical instrument, design a hunting technique, design a water vessel, design a grape press, design a mode of transportation. Any answer is acceptable, no matter how crazy it may seem.

This activity is very appropriate as an introduction to California history.

Mission Wall Words

On the walls of the Sonoma Mission, in large type, are the following words:

1. California's Mission system began at San Diego where Junipero Serra founded San Diego de Alcalá in 1769. Serra saw nine Missions established before his death in 1784.

2. With the padres came the soldiers whose job was to protect the padres, neophytes and settlers. Some settlers brought wives from Mexico and others married Indians.

3. Into the wilderness came the Franciscans; with plow and hoe and churchbell they settled in this new land.

4. From the beginnings of Christianity there have been Missions. California's twenty-one were Catholic. The history of the California Mission is beyond creed or sect. It is part of our heritage.

5. Beginning with bare earth and the padres' zeal, each Mission soon became a walled center of religion and general education for the Indians. Its pastoral husbandry encompassed a vast area of surrounding countryside.

6. California was the Spanish Crown's last frontier in America. Continuing a century old system. The California Missions were a first step toward settlement of this frontier. They were to be followed by pueblos and ranchos.

7. Each Mission was an oasis where the travelers could find safety, repose, and refreshment — a welcome sight in the wilderness.

8. The Mission grew from the very soil upon which it stood. Each had its own plan, following the ancient pattern of strong buildings in a fort-like arrangement about an open compound.

9. With materials native to each area and a few rude tools, the padres taught the Indian converts how to build the Missions. Using redwood, pine, oak, sycamore, soil and stone, they performed incredible feats of construction.

10. The Franciscans left a heritage and a great tribute to their labors. Catholic services have been restored to most of the Missions and they function as churches and schools, except San Francisco Solano and La Purisima Concepcion, which are state historical monuments.

11. Mexico won independence and carried the Spanish idea of secular churches to follow the Missions. Some became villages, churches, some were looted, some abandoned. Most came to a state of ruin.

12. Spaced a day's travel apart, from San Diego to Sonoma, California's Missions have been called "The Golden Chain." Twenty-one were founded between 1769 and 1823.

13. Mission San Francisco Solano — most of its buildings were gone and later the earthquake of 1906 demolished what was left of them. Through the interest and effort of many persons over the past half century, the restoration you see today has been brought about.

Plant Tour

Around even the most urban areas grow many plants used by the natives of California. With a little background information, a short tour or display board could be used to describe some of these native plants and their California Indian uses. Also, an industrious group could begin a native plant use garden.

Suggested references include:
>Balls. *Early Uses of California Plants.*
>Sweet. *Common Edible and Useful Plants of the West.*
>Murphey. *Indian Uses of Native Plants.*

Out of Food?

Make some acorn mush for breakfast, lunch, and dinner.

Grind acorns in a mortar with a pestle; put water into an Indian basket. Drop in some hot rocks for cooking, add acorn meal, and there it is! The Franciscans were so glad to know about this, too, because sometimes they ran out of grains and they couldn't run to the store.

Architecture

Typical design was of a quadrangle, surrounding an open square with an enclosed chapel.

There were quarters for priests, Indians and the Presidio guard *(5-8 men)* — often together.

Kitchen and dining, office, library, workshops, classrooms, storage, laundry, stable, and punishment areas were fairly close together.

Architecture was Iberian and classic, modified, arch and dome, with tile roof, adobe walls, stucco, facade heavy beams. The overhang roofs were used to protect the walls. Embellished facade, windows with glass or parchment, bell tower, well or water storage, and barbecue pit were a part of almost every Mission.

DECORATION

The interior, was usually whitewashed, with wall design paintings, colored tiles, and wrought iron. There were carved pulpits, choir lofts, altars, tabernacles, fonts and water fountains, side chapels besides the main sanctuary of the church.

Religious Items

On display in many Missions are: altar cloths and hangings, priests' vestments, chalice and paten, wafer tongs, wine vessels, tabernacle, candles and candle holders, crucifix, missals, choir books, catechism books, musical instruments and bells, statues and images, paintings of saints and religious allegories, stations of the cross, incense, fireworks for fiestas, and baptismal fonts.

Also frequently displayed are: record books of marriages, baptisms, burials and deaths, etc.; religious books; linguistic books; and libraries.

Mission Processes

Bargaining

Trading can be an interesting activity. Appoint different children to different native or Mission groups and let them figure out where they live, who they might trade with, how far they might travel and the mode of travel, and what was the exchange, etc. Also notice the interesting correlations among Indian trade routes and El Camino Real and the present highway system. Check present harbors with barter ports of the past.

For more information:
> Barrett, Gifford, and Davis. *Trade Routes and Economic Exchange Among the Indians of California.*
> Dana. *Two Years Before the Mast.*

California Indian Baskets

California Indian baskets were made of many kinds of plant materials, from willows for the base and the weaving strands to combinations, including tules, hazels, and red bud.

The basket shape varied from Indian group to Indian group as well as did the decorative pattern.

Baskets were used in the Missions. Their principal functions were for carrying, storing, and cooking. Hot rocks were placed into very tightly woven water-filled baskets, and these rocks heated the water.

As Indian baskets were important in the early years of California, collections can be frequently seen at museum and special exhibits at Missions, Indian sites and other cultural centers.

Maybe you can find a basket maker to share his or her skills with you.

Getting Acquainted

Another creative form of people presentation is in the form of an interview. The group could be interviewing a California Indian. However, a person responding to a prearranged set of questions could be just as successful. Use resource books to provide answers to such questions as: "What is your name?" — "Where do you live?" — "What do you eat?" — "How will you marry?" — "How many folks live in your village?" — "What celebrations do you have?", etc. You will soon find that the children are creating their own questions out of interest and enthusiasm.

Adobe Molds

Molds used for shaping the adobes are made of wood and may be lined with tin for a smooth surface. It prevents any sticking of the soil to the sides. Time will be saved if a double mold is prepared and two bricks can be made in a single operation.

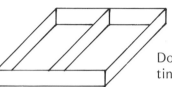

Double mold; wood frame; tin lined

Sun-Dried vs. Burnt Adobe

Some use is made of kiln-fired or burnt adobes. The outstanding advantage of burnt products are: the increased hardness due to the firing and the assurance that a thoroughly dry and very satisfactory adobe may be obtained in a relatively short time. A burnt adobe is very similar in color to an ordinary building brick and is very much harder than a sun-dried product.

Further, if a burnt adobe is left exposed to the natural elements it will remain unchanged for an indefinite period, whereas a sun-dried adobe, if exposed to rain, quickly "melts" and is soon a thin stream of mud. Burnt adobes, then, are resistant to weathering and can be made in a relatively short time.

On the other hand, the sun-dried bricks can be made at slightly less cost and, if coated with plaster, cement, or stucco *(as in common in modern houses)* are not exposed to any weathering, will remain intact for many generations.

Preservation of Meat in Spanish California

Spanish Californians ate meat, but they had no refrigeration, so they preserved it by drying. This dried meat *(usually beef)* was called jerky or charqui.

Soap Making at the Mission

In Mission days, the process to make soap was long because the lye had to be made from ashes and the tallow cut from a steer carcass. The modern method of soap making is as follows:

2½ pounds of tallow and one-half ordinary size can of lye; draw 3/4 pint of water; melt the tallow and then mix lye into water. **CAUTION: DO NOT SPILL LYE AS IT WILL CAUSE BURNS!** Mix lye-water and melted tallow together; stir until it begins to form into into soap. Pour into cookie cans, and let harden. Cut into bars.

The Carreta

The carreta was the cart that carried everything in Spanish California. It was pulled by a donkey, horse, or mule.

Make a carreta of cardboard and paint it as a model.

Mission Cooking

The Mission Fathers were not experienced chefs but they managed the kitchens with the help of Neophytes. Breakfast was early, but probably after Mass. One family member from each Mission compound house came to the kitchen with a bowl and ladle to dish up the daily mush. Those Neophytes who ate at the Missions stood up to eat their mush. In the earliest days it was made from acorns, but wheat or corn were soon permanent substitutes.

Later, coffee or chocolate might be served around noon, but the largest meal was served about 2:00 PM in the dining room of the Mission.

One of the recipes included here might be the main dish. Honey was used instead of sugar. The main flavoring came from *chiles*. *Atole* was frequently served and might be part of *Cena* or supper with *tortillas*. Hot chocolate was the favorite drink.

The Mission Fathers not only prepared meals but raised the produce and animals and processed foods for the table. There were wine presses on the grounds, and slaughter houses from which the cows or sheep were taken at once for the tallow rendering and the hide tanning. Sausages, dried beef, dried corn, figs and apricots, and cheese were among the food stuffs grown and made on the Mission grounds.

While much of this was eaten at the Mission, hides and tallow were used for bartering with trade from the ships from Manila and Boston. The Mission Fathers sowed the seeds that have made California among the nation's largest in wine making, citrus fruit production and cattle raising.

Remember, as Spanish and Mexicans were the first newcomers to California, the earliest recipes are Spanish and Mexican.

Implements for Group Cooking: At home use the pots you have.

> Crock pot: good for beans, rice or pasta soup
> Oven pots
> Skillet: *Tortillas, tacos, tostados; etc.*
> Electric skillet
> Food scales — if you have one available.
> Tortilla holder: Fold a 2 lb. coffee can lid in two; use as a *tortilla* holder when frying *tortilla* in hot grease.

Spanish Mission Implements:

> Wooden bean masher *(potato masher);* knives and boards for cutting *(a blender or food processor);* or lovely carved wooden chocolate mixer *(use slotted spoon);* cast-iron griddle for making *tortillas (electric frying pans and griddles);* Mexican lime squeezer *(orange squeezer, a blender or food processor);* wooden spoons of all sizes and shapes; *metate* and its grinding stone, *la mano* — the *metate* has 3 legs and is made out of rough volcanic rock and is sloping in form; a knife and cutting surface of some sort; a blender or food processor for grinding corn, *chiles* and all of the ingredients for making sauces. *Tortilla* press — or busy hands with a little ball of *Masa con Aqua* — these little balls are patted with hands always at right angles to each other, patting away and changing positions after every pat.

Remember, you can do Mission cooking with only one frying pan, minimum cooking ingredients and 25 to 30 pairs of hands. Don't hesitate to substitute *chiles* — but remember, the seeds and veins are very hot.

Spanish-California Recipes

NIXTAMAL

This is the base of many Mission foods as well as Mexican foods:

tortillas, tamales and tacos.

> 1 gallon water
> 1/3 cup unslaked lime
> 2 quarts *(8 cups)* whole dry corn *(maize)*
> In galvanized kettle, mix the water and lime stirring with a clean stick or a wooden spoon. Add the corn and stir until the mixture no longer bubbles.
> Bring to a boil, then lower the heat so that the mixture cooks but does not boil. Stir frequently. When the skins can be easily rubbed from the kernels *(after about one hour of cooking)* and the corn is moist through, remove from the heat.
> Drain and wash in several changes of cold water until all trace of lime is removed. Rub the kernels between the hands until it is free of hulls.
> You will have a clean corn much like hominy but not so well cooked. This is *nixtamal*, ready to be ground into *masa*.

Lime Water

Quick, or unslaked, lime is used in making the *nixtamal*. The ratio is 1/3 cup lime to 1 gallon water.

MASA

> 1 cup nixtamal
> Water
> Place one cup of *nixtamal* on a *metate;* sprinkle with water to keep it moist. With a small hand-stone, rub back and forth, over and over, until the corn kernels have formed a medium-fine dough. This is *masa.* Cover with a damp cloth to keep from drying.

TORTILLAS

IMPORTANT! The ever delicious *tortilla* now:

> An *ENCHILADA*, fried in oil and all rolled up with filling and sauce;
>
> A *TACO*, fried and folded, filled and sauced;
> A *TOSTADA*, fried, flat, covered and sauced; and
> A *QUESADILLA*, a little cheese, a little heat, and a little *tortilla.*

CORN TORTILLAS

Form the *masa* into 2-inch balls; press and pat with the hand into a 6-inch round cake. Bake on a hot, ungreased griddle until slightly brown and blistered on both sides.

Wheat Tortillas (Tortillas De Trigo)

> 2 cups *harina de trigo* (wheat)
> ¼ lb. lard or ½ lb. vegetable shortening
> 2 tsp. salt
> 1 cup warm water
>
> Knead mixture for 3 minutes; set it aside for 3 hours before cooking.

MAKING THE ENCHILADAS

> 12 *tortillas*
> 3 cups filling
> 4 cups sauce, heated
> 1 cup chopped onion
> 2 cups grated cheese, jack or yellow
> Oil for frying *tortillas*, 1" in 8" frying pan.
>
> Heat oil. Dip *tortilla* in hot oil, press down for a few seconds, turn, press, remove and drain. Continue until all *tortillas* done.
>
> Put a little sauce into oblong baking dishes. The 13" x 8" will hold 8 enchiladas. It is important to not crowd them. Bathe *tortilla* in this sauce, turning to moisten both sides. Place about 2 tablespoons filling in center, roll and leave in pan, seam side down. When

pan full, add more sauce, sprinkle with grated cheese and put in 375º oven to melt cheese. Before serving, sprinkle with raw chopped onion.

FILLINGS FOR ENCHILADAS

Beef Enchilada
    1 tablespoon oil
    ½ cup chopped onion
    2 lbs. hamburger, preferably coarse ground
    Salt and pepper to taste
    3 tsp. oregano, crushed
    1 cup peeled tomatoes, optional

Heat oil. Saute onion until soft. Add meat and seasoning. Cook 10 minutes. Drain off excess grease. Add tomato and cook another 5 minutes until meat is done. Fill *tortilla* and proceed as for other *enchiladas.*

TACOS

    12 *tortillas*
    3 cups lettuce, shredded
    1 large tomato, sliced
    1 large avocado, sliced
    1 cup Cheddar cheese, shredded
    ½ pint sour cream
    Pickled *chiles* to taste
    Bottled green *taco* sauce to taste

Drop *tortillas* in hot oil, one at a time. After a few seconds turn, fold in half, and fry to desired crispness. Drain on paper towels and keep warm in a low-heat oven. To serve, open each *tortilla* gently and let each person select his own condiments. Serves 6.

TOSTADAS

    8 *tortillas*
    Oil for frying
    2 cups refried beans
    2 cups meat filling
    2 cups shredded lettuce
    2 sliced tomatoes
    1 large avocado
    ½ cup Parmesan cheese
    1 pint sour cream
    8 ripe olives, sliced
    Pickled *chile* slices

Fry *tortillas* on both sides in hot oil until crisp. Drain on paper towels. Spread *tortillas* generously with refried beans, then meat filling; add lettuce, tomato, and avocado. Sprinkle with Parmesan cheese, top with sour cream, pickled *chile* slices and olives. Serves 4.

QUESADILLAS

You can vary this recipe by adding beans, meat, onion, and/or garlic.

    1½ cups Monterey Jack cheese, shredded *(or Cheddar cheese)*
    6 Tbsp. green *chiles,* chopped
    6 *tortillas*
    Salt
    Oil for frying

Put ¼ cup cheese and 1 tbsp. *chiles* on half of each *tortilla;* sprinkle each with salt. Heat a small amount of oil in a frying pan, and put the *tortillas* in, one at a time, without folding. Fry for a few seconds. Fold the *tortillas* over the filling, press the edges together. Fry on both sides until crisp. Drain on paper towel before serving. Makes 6.

ATOLE

This is a thick, hot drink, not unlike thin mush. It is enjoyed all over Mexico today as it was in the past. It was a favorite for Mission Fathers and Indians. There are many ways to make it: Mix a cup of corn flour *(masa)* or rice flour with 2 cups of cold water and a pinch of salt. To this add 2 cups of boiling water. Cook it oh, so slowly; for 1 hour.

For plain *atole* — Serve as is.
For spicy *atole* — add a little *chile.*
For fruit *atole* — add some fresh or canned fruit
For sweet *atole* — add a little brown sugar with cinnamon
For chocolate *atole* — add cinnamon, sugar and grated Mexican or bitter chocolate to the *atole* and you have and you made *champurrados* — or a "full bodied" hot chocolate.

Hot chocolate was very popular among Mission Members, Neophytes and Priests alike:
Chocolate beaters are available in Mexican food stores — they were used to fluff up chocolate cocoa. The chocolate was brought from Mexico on trading ships — squares of bitter chocolate are second to Mexico's own sweet chocolate "rounds." Milk, eggs, sugar, cinnamon can all be used in making Mexican hot chocolate.

SOPA DE CALABAZA

Pumpkin Soup

    3 tablespoons lard
    ½ cup chopped onion
    2 cloves garlic, crushed
    2 tablespoons flour
    3 cups chicken broth
    2 cups milk
    2 cups cooked, pureed pumpkin or Hubbard
    or Acorn Squash
    1 cup whole kernel corn
    1 tsp ground cumin
    1 tsp salt
    ½ tsp pepper
    1 egg yolk
    1 cup cream
    ½ cup sherry
    1 cup sour cream
    1 cup toasted pumpkin seeds

Heat lard. Saute onion and garlic. Blend in flour. Add broth and stir until thickened. Add milk. Bring to boil. Lower heat or transfer to double boiler. Add pumpkin, corn and seasonings. Cook 20 minutes uncovered.

Beat yolk and cream. Add a little hot mixture, then then transfer to soup, beating with whisk until thickened, about 3 minutes. Add sherry.

Pour in bowls and top with sour cream and a sprinkling of pumpkin seeds.

EMPAÑADAS

These were made frequently in the Missions.

    2 cups flour
    2 tsp baking powder
    1 tsp salt
    ½ cup shortening
    1/3 cup ice water
    Oil for frying

Sift flour with baking powder and salt, and cut shortening in with a pastry blender. Add water and knead lightly.

Divide mixture into 12 balls; roll each into a circle 1/8 inch thick. Put 1 spoonful of filling on half of each circle. Moisten edges of circles with water, fold over the filling, and press the edges together. Press fork tines around the edges. Bake in 400° oven for 20 minutes, until golden brown or fry in hot oil (300) until golden, and drain on paper towels. Makes 12.

TAMALES

Husks are sold by the pound. For 2 dozen *tamales* allow about 4 oz. Soak them in very hot water for about 15 minutes or until pliable. Separate the husks. Remove any corn silk, and wrap in a towel to dry. Foil may be used instead of husks. It is easier to handle the *tamales* if they are wrapped in cooking parchment paper even though they are in husks.

MASA *(the dough)*

    3 cups *masa harina (prepared flour for making tortillas, etc.)*
    1 cup shortening
    2 cups chicken or pork broth, tepid
    1 tsp. salt

Cream the shortening. Add part of the *masa harina* and salt. Cream. Add liquid then rest of *masa harina.* Beat until very fluffy. When sufficiently beaten a small ball of the dough will float in water.

Making the Tamales

Choose largest of the husks, or put two together, cementing them with a little of the dough. Be sure husk isn't too wet or the *masa* will not stick.

Spread a thick layer of *masa* on the wide end. Leave the pointed end empty. Put a generous spoonful of the red or green sauce on the *masa* and spread it. Put pieces of chicken, pork or beef or cheese *(shredded)* in center. Bring the two sides over, loosely. Turn up the pointed end. Tie with strip of husk or wrap in parchment paper, twisting the bottom end. Keep as nearly upright as possible.

TAMALE FILLINGS

Chicken Tamales

3 cups cooked chicken shredded very coarsely. 3 cups *salsa colorada,* preferably the one made with dried *chiles,* and cut the liquid down to 1 cup tomato sauce and 1½ cups water. Also add more cumin. If use the *salsa colorada* made with *chile* powder, thicken it with flour.

Pork Tamales

3 cups cooked pork in fairly large pieces 3 or 4 cups *salsa verde* made a little thicker by using little or no extra water.

Beef Tamales

3 cups shredded cooked beef 3 or 4 cups *salsa verde or salsa colorada.*

To fill the *tamale,* spread sauce over dough, then put in pieces of meat or fowl, then add more sauce. When it comes to serving, open up the *tamale* but leave it sitting on the husk. Add more sauce, kept aside for this purpose, and heated. Recipes for 12 *tamales.*

Variations: Instead of adding more *salsa colorada*

To fill the *tamale,* spread sauce over dough, then put in pieces of meat or fowl, then add more sauce. When it comes to serving, open up the *tamale*

Variations: Instead of adding more *salsa colorada* when serving, it is nice to top with *chili beans.* Cook beans as usual, rinse, then mix with *salsa colorado,* extra onions and cooked hamburger, if desired.

Add peanuts or almonds and/or raisins to the basic meat or chicken *tamale* recipes for a change of texture and taste.

COOKING THE TAMALES

The *tamales* must steam about 1½ to 2 hours in a kettle with a tight fitting lid. The kettle must be deep enough to hold about 2'' of water below the rack on which tamales are placed. The *tamales* should be standing upright and the water must not touch them, but they must be arranged loosely so that the steam circulates around them. Put hot water in the kettle and place the rack so the water is below it. Arrange the *tamales* standing up on the folded end or twisted end if parchment paper is used. Put a cloth over the top of the kettle with the lid on top of the cloth. Keep the water boiling gently. Add water, if necessary, so that it won't boil dry. At the end of 1½ hours, take out a *tamale,* and unroll. If it is cooked the dough will come away from the husk and look and taste cooked. When serving the *tamale,* take off paper if paper is used, unroll husk and fold back under *tamale.* It is well to have some extra sauce hot to pour over the *tamale.*

SALSA COLORADA   Using *Chile* Powder

2 tablespoons lard
8 tablespoons *chile* powder
1 cup tomato sauce
3 cups water
1 tsp sugar
½ tsp ground cinnamon
Salt to taste

Melt lard. Add *chile* powder and cook, stirring, a few seconds. Add tomato sauce, simmer a minute or two. Add water and seasonings. Cook 10 to 15 minutes.

Taste for seasoning. You may wish to add more *chile* powder, or more cumin. The different brands of *chile* powder vary. When you have found one you like you will know what to add.

The *salsa colorada* made with the dried *chiles* has more body and seems to go farther. If you are making 12 *enchiladas* using the *chile* powder you might do well to increase the *chile* powder by 2 tablespoons and add 1 cup more water and 1 cup tomato sauce.

BUNUELOS   Traditional Mission Dessert

Makes about 3 dozen

> 2 cups flour
> ¼ cup sugar
> 1 tsp. baking powder
> 1 egg
> 1/3 cup milk
> 2 tbsp. melted butter

Sift dry ingredients together. Beat egg and milk together. Add to dry ingredients. Add melted butter and mix well. Turn out on floured board and knead a few times. Wrap and chill if possible. Pinch off pieces about the size of a walnut. Roll into smooth balls. Roll out very thin, paper thin. Each one should be about 5" or 6" round. It is best to roll out all the *bunuelos*, stacking with paper between before you begin to fry them. Have oil very hot. Drop *bunuelo* in, turn, then turn again if not brown. Drain well on absorbent paper. While still hot, sprinkle with cinnamon and sugar. Traditionally they are served broken into bowls with Piloncillo syrup, and eaten with the fingers.

MEXICAN HOT CHOCOLATE

> 2 cups boiling water or 2 cups scalded milk
> 3 ounces Mexican chocolate, broken into small pieces

In a small heavy saucepan bring water to boil; stir in chocolate; mix over low heat, stirring until the chocolate is melted. Pour the mixture into an earthenware pitcher and whip it to a froth with a wooden *molinillo* or mix in blender for 2 to 3 seconds until frothy. Add cinnamon to make it fit for a party. Serves 2.

POZOLE — PORK AND HOMINY STEW

> 1 lb. pork neck bones
> 2 quarts chicken broth
> ½ cup chopped onion
> 3 or 4 cloves garlic
> 3 lbs pork cut in 1" cubes
> 6 oz. dried California *chiles* (about 12 pods)
> or 6 tbsp. *chile* powder
> 2 cups white hominy
> 1 cup cooked beans *(use ½ cup kidney beans cooked in 3 cups water.)*
> Salt and pepper to taste

In large kettle cook neck bones in chicken broth, with onion and garlic, for about 2 hours. Remove neck bones, cut off meat, and return to kettle. Add pork cubes. Cook 45 minutes.

Remove seeds and veins from dried *chiles*. Soak in boiling water about 20 minutes. Drain. Puree.

At end of 45 minutes test to see if pork is done. Continue cooking if pork cubes are not tender. Add the pureed *chiles* (or *chile powder*), hominy, salt and pepper. Cook 15 minutes.

Serve in bowls with side dishes of:
> chopped onions
> oregano
> lemon wedges
> sliced radishes
> salsa picante
> shredded lettuce
> chili pepper flakes

POZOLE (VEGETARIAN)

Early California Style

> 1 small onion, chopped
> 2 garlic cloves, chopped
> Saute in:
> 1 tbsp. oil
> Until brown, then add:
> 3 cups water or broth
> ½ cup raw kidney beans, washed
> ½ cup raw whole wheat berries or whole rye berries
> 1 tsp. mixed herbs
> ½ tsp. mustard seeds or mustard powder
> ¼ tsp. salt
> ¼ tsp. black pepper

Bring to boil; then cover and simmer for 1½ to 2 hours until tender. Add 3 to 4 large leaves of swiss chard, coarsely cut. Simmer about 10 minutes, until tender. Serves 2.

Vinegar — Put 2 gallons fresh water, a pint of dark molasses, and a dissolved yeastcake or powdered yeast packet all together in a wooden vat; cover with a thin sheet of cotton and Eureka! — in 3 or 4 weeks you'll have vinegar.

Spanish-English Dictionary (Glossary) for Spanish California

This might be called a starter glossary and can be reproduced for each user. As new Spanish words or the names of places are discovered, they may be added to this list.

If at all possible, have a Spanish-English Dictionary close at hand. They are available in libraries and inexpensive in book stores.

AN EVERYBODY GETS A COPY — GLOSSARY-DICTIONARY

The list of Spanish words chosen for inclusion in this glossary is far from complete. The words that are listed are frequently used Spanish words and many of these words pepper our state as the names of places.

SPANISH ALPHABET:

a b c ch d e f g h i j k l ll m n ñ o p r rr s t u v w x y z

Some Pronounciation Hints:

a = ah	e = ay as in May
i = ee, as in see	o = o as in low
u = oo as in moo	ch = ch as in choo choo train

rr = roll your r so you sound like an airplane just taking off or about ready to land
ll = ya   ñ = like the n in Tanya

WRITTEN NUMBERS FROM 1 TO 20

uno, dos, tres, cuatro, cinco, seis, siete, ocho, nueve, diez, once, doce, trece, catorce, quince, diez y seis *(y means "and")*, diez y siete, diez y ocho, diez y nueve, veinte.

NAMES OF THE MONTHS

enero, febrero, marzo, abril, mayo, junio, julio, agosto, septiembre, octobre, noviembre, diciembre.

DAYS OF THE WEEK

domingo, lunes, martes, miércoles, jueves, viernes, sábado.

Adobe — special mud and straw mixture *(formed in a mold and dried in the sun or in an oven.)*

Agua — water; Agua caliente means hot water *(guess what the word is for hot)*

Ajo — garlic

Alabanzo — the name of a Catholic song of praise, (alabado = praised)

Alba — morning prayer at the mission

Alameda — grove of poplar trees. Alameda is the name of a city, a county and many streets. Maybe you live on an Alameda.

Alamo —poplar tree: In California it is called the cottonwood tree. Alamo is the name of cities, streets, and schools, to name a few.

Alcatraz — Easter lily. Alcatraz was the name of a famous federal prison in San Francisco Bay.

Alhambra — a Moorish estate in Granada, Spain. The name of valleys, a city, streets and avenues in California.

Alto — high; upper; tall as "upper California" is higher up on the map than Baja California.

Amador — lover; sweetheart; Amador County, family, valley and town are all in California. Also, a man's name.

Amigo — friend

Ana — Santa Ana is a city near Disneyland. *(Ann, in English. St. Ann was mother of Mary, mother of Christ)*

Andreas — Saint Andrew; spelled "Andrés" a valley and an earthquake faultline.

Angel — angel; Los Angeles — The Angeles; short form of the city, El Puebla de Nuestra; Señora La Reina de Los Angeles, "Our Lady the Queen of Angeles;" California's largest city.

Antonio — San Antonio; Saint Anthony; a place, a ship, a name and a mission.

Anza — a Spanish explorer and expedition leader; also the name of a street; a desert, a park, and a train and a school or two.

Bahía — bay

Baja — lower; Baja California

Baño — bath; Los Baños — a bathing place of priests in earlier times; a city in California's cotton-farming country.

Bárbara — saint from Rome, Italy; in California: — a mission, Santa Barbara Channel Islands; a city; a county; the name of one of this book's authors.

Barata — to barter and/or exchange; tallow and hides were used as barter for needed goods. These were brought from the far east and the Eastern United States.

Barato — cheap; inexpensive

Barca — a little boat made from tules, or just a little boat.

Barrio — a district in a city or town.

Bautista — baptizer; San Juan Bautista, "Saint John the Baptist;" name of a mission and a city, at least.

Bela — candle

Bella — beautiful; many names of places contain this this word, such as Bella Vista which means " "beautiful view."

Bernadino — Saint Bernadette; a city and county named San Bernadino

Bienvenido — welcome

Boca — mouth, such as the mouth of a person, a bay, or a river.

Bolinas — an Indian name of a place.

Bolsa — pocket or purse; When the rancho period was in full swing, this word was often used to describe "a little piece of land."

Bonito — pretty; bonita; descriptive word or name of many pretty places.

Bota — a leather water or wine container.

Brea — tar, as in La Brea Tar Pits in Southern California.

Buena — good.

Buena Ventura — a good venture and the name of the 9th mission

Burro — beasts of burden; the original "carry-alls."

Caballero — horseman or gentleman

Caballo — horse

Cabra — goat

Cabrillo — a little goat; Cabrillo — name of California's early explorer.

Calabaza — squash

Calavera — skulls; the word Calaveras is the name of a California county.

Camino — Road; journey

Camino Real — King's Highway (real means "royal") "royal") which links the missions

Camino Alto — high road; the name of several streets.

Cañada — canyon; La Cañada is a town.

Carlos — Charles; El Rey Carlos de Espana (King Charles of Spain)

Cebolla — onion

Carpentería — Carpenter's shop; Carpenteria is a town near Santa Barbara.

Carta — letter; Write one to your favorite mission today and, if you want an answer, be sure to put in a stamped, self addressed envelope.

Casa — house; casa grande — a large house; Casa Grande is a town.

Cerrito — a small hill; El Cerrito is a town in California

Chícharos — peas

Chico — young; Chico is a city in California.

Chiles — a very spicy vegetable used in Mexican cooking.

Chula Vista — a place in California; chula is beautiful or oh, so cute.

Cojo — a lame person; Cojo Point is a special valley.

Colorado — reddish; Colorado is a river and desert, also a state.

Comida — noon dinner

Conejo — rabbit; El Conejo is a rancho, a creek, and a mountain.

Coyote — a little North American wolf; Coyote River Canyon is a specific place.

Cruz — cross; Santa Cruz is the name of a city and county.

Cuesta — a hill.

Delgado — thin; Delgado Point is the name of a place. place.

Diablo — devil; evil; Diablo is a mountain; a college; and a valley.

San Diego — named for Saint Didacus. Say it fast 10 times and see if you can make it sound like San Diego!

Divisadero — a divider; Divisadero is a street name in San Francisco.

Dolor — pain; sorrow. Mission Dolores is often used as a substitute name for "Mission San Francisco de Asís."

Don — sir

Doña — madam

Dorado — golden; Eldorado is a county. You may find it in other places, such as on street signs.

El — the singular masculine article.

Estado — state

España — Spain

Fandango — Spanish dance

Felicidad — happiness; Felicidad is the name of a town.

Fierro — cattle brand to show ownership.

Fiesta — party; celebration; festival; holiday.

Flaco — thin

Flecha — arrow

Flor — flower; Las Flores is the name of many streets.

Fresa — flower; Las Flores is the name of many streets.

Fresno — strawberry

Fraile — friar; often used for priest

Frijoles — beans

Frío — cold

Fruta — fruit

Fuego — fire

Gallina — hen

Gallo — rooster

Garrote — house; capital punishment by hanging

Gato — cat; Los Gatos *(the cats)* is the name of a town.

Gaucho — herdsman or man of humble birth; later it seemed to mean "cowboy" in Argentina.

Gaviota — seagull; Gaviota Granada is the name of a town.

Guerra — war

Hacienda — large ranch

Hambre — hunger

Helado — ice cream

Hermana — sister

Hermano   brother

Higo — fig

Hombre — man

Horno   oven

Hornito (hornillo) — earth oven where Mexicans baked their bread; little oven.

Indio — Indian; Indio is a town in the desert area of California.

Santa Inés — Saint Agnes; A Mission and a river bear her name.

Isla — island

-ito, -illo — endings often put on the end of Spanish words to show that they are little or cute.

Jabón — soap

Jacinto — hyacinth; San Jacinto *(Saint Hyacinth; many mountains and ranchos are named for him.)*

Jardín — garden

Jitomate — tomato

Joachín — a name from Catholic history; The name of a county, river, and valley.

La Jolla — the jewel; often mispronounced "joy a;" La Jolla is a city near San Diego. Should be spelled "La Joya."

José — Joseph; San Jose; Saint Joseph; San Jose is a city, and a Mission.

Juan Bautista — John the Baptist; Mission San Juan Bautista

Juan Capistrano — John; Mission San Juan Capistrano

Juego — game

La — the; singular, feminine article

Lago — lake

Laguna — small lake; Laguna Beach is a city.

Luís — Louis.

Madero — wood; Madera County.

Madre — mother

Malo — bad

Manteca — tallow; lard

Manzana — apple

Manzanita — little apple; reddish barked bush with red berries shaped like little apples.

Marina — adjective = marine; shore or coast; Marin may be the shortened form, as in Marin County, just north of the Golden Gate Bridge; and the home of Mission San Rafael. Small harbor for boats.

Marinero — sailor

Mayordomo — person in charge of vaqueros or cowboys

Mesa — table; level hill

Mestizo — a person containing Indian and Spanish or other European blood.

Metate — Indian grinding stone; this is like a mortar and pestle, which is a round grinding rock with rock instrument to do the grinding; used by the Indians.

Miguel — Michael; San Miguel — a saint, a mission, and a little town.

Modesto — modest; Modesto is the name of a city

Montar — to ride horseback.

Monte — mountain; used in naming many places, such as El Monte; Montecito *(see how many streets, little towns or big towns have this as their first word).*

Morro — animal snout or round hill; headland; cliff; Morro Bay and rock.

Muerto — dead; also used in the names of places hither and thither

Mujer — woman

Nacimiento — birth; name of a river and a canyon

Nada — nothing; Nada is a place, too.

Naranja — Orange

Natividad — the birth of Christ at Christmas. Also Navidad.

Nevada — snow-covered; the Sierra Nevada mountain range; Nevada County and the state of Nevada.

Niño — child

Noche — night

Noche buena — good night or Christmas.

Novato — a beginner; Novato is a town.

Nuestra — our

Nueva — new

Nuez — nut; especially pecan.

Obispo — bishop

Océana — ocean

Ojai — an Indian place name and a city near Santa Barbara.

Ojos — eyes

Olivero — basket for carrying olive from harvest to storage.

Olivo — olive or olive tree.

Olvera — a Spanish — California leader and a famous street in Los Angeles.

Pablo — Paul; San Pablo — Saint Paul; a bay and a city.

Pacífico — peaceful; our ocean's name.

Padre — father; priest; Los Padres — a national forest near Santa Barbara.

Pais — country

Pájaro — bird; Pajaro is a river and a valley.

Palo — stick; Palos Verde — Green Stick; Palo Alto is a city.

Paso —pass; passage; Paso Robles — Pass of the Oaks.

Piñata — a clay pot usually decorated with paper frills and filled with goodies for parties.

Piñón — pine nuts; the name of a place or two; Pinon Point; Punta de Pinon

Pismo — Indian place word meaning tar.

Playa — beach; Playa Del Rey is a place and the name of a beach; beach of the king.

Plumas — feather or a pen *(remember, they used to use feathers as pens);* There is a county named Plumas and a river named Feather. Now that's a switch!

Portola, Gaspar — the Spanish commander of the expedition that explored and colonized California; a city, valley, street, and maybe more. Look for this name in your community.

Potrero — a field that was or is used as a pasture for horses. You'll see it on street signs in a few cities.

Presidio — military location.

Pueblo — village

Pulga — flea; There must have been lots of early scratchers because streets and valleys and other places have Pulga in their names.

Punta — point; The early namers used this. See how many puntas there are in your area.

Purísima — purest; Mission La Purísima was named for Mary, the mother of Jesus.

Queso — cheese

Rafael — St. Raphael the Archangel; his name was used for a Mission, a city and a rancho.

Rancho — ranch really refers to the big cattle - raising ranchos during the cattle raising days of Spanish and Indian California; started, of course, by the Mission founders.

Rata — rat

Real — royal; later, when we were not under "royal or kingly" rule this meant "open." El Camino Real was named the King's Highway by the Spanish who had a king but now the "kingly" meaning is lsot in a lovely sea of democracy.

Redondo — round; Redondo Beach must be a round beach!

Refugio — refuge; shelter; Refugio is at least the name of one rancho and one playa or beach.

Reina — queen

Represa — repressed; the name of the post office for the prison and town of Folsom; a small dam.

Rey — king

Rincón — corner

Río — river; name of towns on river banks, creeks, and rivers. Be on a "rio" search!

Rodeo — a cattle roundup; today a rodeo often is a great big show including competitions, contests, etc., for the public, showing cows, steer, horses, etc. at their show-off best; it still means a cattle roundup.

Rosa — rose; Santa Rosa was a Peruvian saint and is the name of a city and other palce names.

Rubio — blonde

Sacramento — sacramento; Sacramento is the name of California's capital city; a county; and a river.

La Sala — living room

Salina — a salt pit or marsh; Salinas is a city, a river, and a valley near Carmel and Monterey.

Sandía — watermelon

Santa — Saint

Sausalito — little willow grove; Sausalito is the name of a Golden Gate Bridge town, possibly taken from little willow.

Seguro — safe; sure

Señor — sir; gentleman; mister.

Señora — mistress; lady; madam

Sepulveda — name of many locations, i.e., pass, boulevard; Sepulveda is a Spanish surname.

Serra, Junipero — the first President of the California Mission System and a highway.

Silla — chair

Silla de Montar — saddle

Sitio — location

Socorro — help

Sobrante — left over; El Sobrante is a place near San Francisco built on extra land.

Solano — a place with lots of sun; name of an Indian chief and the name of a county; Mission San Francisco Solano in Sonoma County.

Soldado — soldier

Soledad — solitude; Soledad is the name of a city and prison; Mission Nuestra Senora de la Soledad.

Sombrero — a large brimmed hat.

Sonoma — an Indian name for General Vallejo's settlement; a county; city and a state park.

Sueño — sleep; dream.

Sur — south; Big Sur.

Tamal — name of Indian tribe.

Tamal País — country of the Indian tribes; pais means country. A mountain.

Tejón — badger; El Tejon is a specific pass and a canyon.

Temblor — earthquake

Término — end

Tía — aunt

Tío — uncle

Tiburón — shark; Tiburon is a peninsula, ranch and a town on the San Francisco Bay.

Tierra — land or earth.

Timoteo — Timothy; San Timoteo — Saint Timothy; Marin County Land Grant

Trinidad — trinity; Trinidad is a bay, a town, a county, and a river.

Triunfo — triumph; Triunfo is a canyon and a pass.

Trocar — to barter and/or exchange; tallow and hides were used as barter for needed goods. These were brought from the far east and the Eastern United States.

Tulare — a grove of bullrushes; Tulare is a city and county.

Tuna — a prickly pear cactus.

Último — last

Un — one (masculine - adjective form)
     noun = uno.

Una — one (feminine)

Usted — you

Uva — grape; name of a canyon and the "Grapevine" is the name of a curvy highway.

Vaca — cow; name of a Spanish family; Vacaville — cow city

Valle — valley; the big central valley was named el valle grande.

Vallecito or Vallejo — a little valley; Vallejo — a Mexican military leader and land owner; the name of a city usually said Valeho.

Vaquero — cowboy

Vega — open plain

Vela — candle

Venida — arrival

Venta — sale

Ventana — window

Ventura — fortune or luck; Mission Buena Ventura

Verdad — truth

Verde — green; Verde appears in the names of many California places.

Viento — wind

Villa — village or country house.

Visitación — Visitation; Visitacion is a rancho and a valley.

Vista — view; part of the names of many places, i.e., Vista del Mar is "view of the sea;" Linda Vista is "beautiful view."

Viva — long live; hurrah.

W — No initial "w" in Spanish.

Yerba — herb; Yerba buena is "good herb;" name of a place and an island in San Francisco Bay.

Bibliography

Chevron School Broadcast
The Story of the California Missions — 1983.
Mission line drawings, a tape and beautiful film strip comprise this packet made and given for each elementary school in California. Ed Franklin produced this fine family of teaching aids. Use this at school for Indian or Mission introduction. Use the film strip with and without the tape and vice-versa. Note, especially, the beautiful Indian portraits from the Bancroft Library. This group will serve you well at school.

Arillaga. *Diary of His Surveys of the Frontier-1766.* Translated into English — 1969.

Auto Club of Southern California. *Baja California.* Available through the California AAA.

Barton, Bruce. *A Tree in the Center of the World.* Ross Erickson. Adult. Very complete volume on the Missions with charming folk tales used hither and yon to make the time come to life. Do have a copy around.

Bauer, Helen. *California Mission Days.* Doubleday & Co. Good children's book on the settling, working in, and living in the California Missions. This book is so complete that it serves all ages.

Bauer, Helen. *California Rancho Days.* Doubleday & Co. All ages. Manner of rancho acquisition discussed together with the mode of rancho life. Particular "features" of a number of separate ranchos are delightfully dealt with; a good glossary and a "Rancho Guide Table" is available for use.

Bernstein, Margery and Krobin, Janet. *Earth Namer.* Charles Scribner & Sons. A California Indian myth.

Biggs, Donald. *Conquer and Colonize.* Presidio Press. Level: adult and gifted children.

Castor, Henry. *The First Book of The Spanish-American West.* Albert Micale, Illustrator. Level: 4th grade to adult. Wonderful pictures show the Indians and their successors, the explorers. The missionaries, the "support groups" of Spanish California are put into the total context of the history of California.

Copely, James. *The Call to California.* Union Tribune Publishing Co. Level: grades 7 and up. This book tells the story of the 1769 Portola/Serra expedition. Father Crespi's delightful diary is tucked in bits and pieces to set the work on fire a bit. This book is beautifully illsutrated and is amost a resource must.

Dana, Richard Henry Jr. *Two Years Before the Mast.* A personal history. This is truly a classic and offers the reader fine literature and craftsmanship, compelling descriptions of life on and off a Boston trading ship. Bartering on the Spanish-California Coast comes to life.

DaSilva, Owen Francis. *Music of California.* The Mission Fathers discovered a delightful method of instructing Mission Indians in part singing,through the use of colored music notes. Mission Santa Barbara houses many of these lovely sheets and Father DaSilva was the real Mission musicologist.

de Angulo, Jaime. *Indian Tales.* Hill and Wang.

Duffus, R.L. and Norton. *Queen Calafia's Island.* Level: easy adult. Fine background reading with legend and fact,placing Spanish Alta and California missionaries in the totality of the state's earliest footsteps until today. *Queen Calafia* is a very fitting title as we glimpse into the whys and whatfors of naming the state. This book lacks bibliography and an index.

Englehardt. *The Franciscan sof California. Missions and Missionaries of California.* A dedicated researcher and author. Level: adult. Probably the best work,certainly up to its publication in 1916. You can learn a lot from Father Engelhardt.

Geiger, Maynard. *Life and Times of Father Junipero Serra.* This is another classic resource book written by a Franciscan. It deals fully with the Missions and Father Serra.

Hawthorne, Hidegard. *California's Missions: Their Romance and Beauty.* Level: adult. This doesn't belie the title for indeed this "romance" may have more "glitter" today than at the time of their founding. A book to catch you up in all the best of Spanish California.

Heizer & Elasser. *The Natural World of the California Indian.* U.C. Press. Adult. The book is divided into topic areas which are then dealt with regionally. This contains excellent background reading.

Hutchinson, W.H. *California the Golden Shore by the Sundown Sea.* This is a very complete paperback history of California. Spanish California is discussed fully and is like a diamond in taking its place in a bracelet. It neither dominates nor is dominated by any other historical era. This is a real ready reference.

Jackson, Helen Hunt. *Ramona. Father Junipero Serra and the Mission Indians. Glimpses of California and the Missions.* Little, Brown. 1902. The first two of these and the Mission Collection of little Mission stories are literary classics of the time, but surprisingly, if used alone, today would evoke much controversy, i.e., could be a maudlin approach to those "precious" Missions and missionaries.

Karney. *The Listening One.* John Day. For children. This is the story of a California Mission Indian girl. It is the story of her tasks, her life, her struggles and her victories. It is set in the background of the Spanish-Mexican struggle over California.

Leeper, Vera. *Indian Legends Live In Puppetry.* Naturegraph. A creative manual.

Lewis, Oscar. *The Story of California.* Doubleday. Level: grade 4 and up. The chapter headings: Discovery; Drake and the Golden Hinde; Manila Galleons; Trail-Breakers; Missions and Ranchos; The Coming of Foreigners; etc. give an indication of the scope of this work. This book is well conceived, well written and illustrated and gives a good background.

Marinacci. *California's Spanish Place Names.* Presidio Press. All ages. This is a charming book that bounces the reader all over California on street and highway signs. Little stories perk up the reader's understanding of the Spanish starter words in California.

Martinez, Pablo L. *A History of Lower California.* An English translation.

Michaelis, John. *Social Studies for Children in a Democratic Society.* Prentice Hall. Dr. Michaelis gives the reader a solid, worthwhile foundation on which to place the social studies education of our K-12 population. Keep a copy at your elbows.

Newcomb, Rexford. *The Old Mission Churches and Historic Houses of California.* Lippincott. Level: adult. This is a treasury of Mission and Mission style architecture. It doesn't simply present the reader with examples and descriptions but expands to include sound arguments for Mission Architecture in California.

Palver, Francisco. *Founding the First California Mission.* Nurvena California Press. Level: adult. This is truly an "I was there" account of the founding of the early Missions. Good primary source material.

Reed and Orze. *Art from Scrap.* Davis Publications. This is a great budget helper filled with no or low cost ideas for masks and puppet making, maps, invitations to Mission programs. Take a peek for idea sparking and some thrift "Mission Innovations" of your own.

Van Allen & Allen. *Language Experience Activities.* Houghton-Mifflin. This book is fitted with worthwhile activities designed to benefit the learner's language art skills. It will also deepen his understanding of the content under scrutiny. An example here might be "using a publishing center" as described in the book for Mission history. This is a good parent-teacher book.

Robertson. *Baja California and Its Missions.*

Rush, Phillip. *Some Old Ranchos and Adobes.* Level: adult or gifted. A number of these "early sites" are described in detail. Differences and similarities of many ranchos are pinpointed. Good readong for the history buff.

Scott. *Junipero Serra — A Pioneer of the Cross.* Valley Pub. This is for children. It is the story of the boy who became the man who started our California Mission system.

Sunset. *The California Missions.* Land Publishing. This is an outstanding book, from exploration to secularization. It is very complete and is recommended as a general reference book on the Missions.

Towendolly, Grant (tales told to) Masson, Marcelle. *A Bag of Bones.* Naturegraph. Legends of the Wintu Indians of Northern California.

Wheelock and Guillock. *Baja California Guidebook — 1975.* Clark. The authors have included sections on the history and geography of Baja as well as sections on travel and plant and animal life.

Herbs — *Mission San Antonio Padua.* This is a delightful booklet with pen and ink drawings of plants which are listed in latin. Their descriptions are given quite fully. Booklet available at the Mission, Jolon, CA *(enclose $5.95 for cost and handling).*

Arts and Crafts Books

Arts and Crafts for All Seasons, Linse *(Pitman)*

The Crayon, Horn *(Davis)*
A helpful book with ways to use crayons to give good and varied effect.

Paper Construction for Children. Krevitsky *(Rheinhold)*
This book can point your way to Mission people, animals, and growing things with paper construction.

Weaving Without a Loom, Rainy *(Davis)*

The Art of Papier Maché, Kenny *(Chilten)*

Creative Clay Design, Rottger *(Rheinhold)*

Creating with Paper, Johnston *(University of Washington)*
Two or three dimension paper art, adaptable in many ways.

Puppet Making Through the Grades, Hooper *(Davis)*
This shows a host of ideas beyond those here in this book.

Making Things, Wiseman *(Little Brown)*

Mask Making, Baranski *(Davis)*

Cook Books

California Mission Recipes, Cleveland, Bess *(Tuttle)*

Mexican Cook Book, Sunset *(Lane Books, Menlo Park, CA)*

The Cuisines of Mexico, Kennedy, Diana *(Harper and Row)*

The Tortilla Book, Kennedy, Diana *(Harper and Row)*

Latin American Cooking, *(Time-Life Books)*

30 Mexican Menus, Stone, Idella Purnell *(The Ward Ritchie Press)*

The Complete Book of Mexican Cooking, Ortiz, Elizabeth Lambert *(Bantam)*

The Mexican Cook, Wallace, George & Inger *(Nitty Gritty Prod.)*

Mexican Cooking, Fisher, Kathleen Dunning *(Grosset & Dunlap)*

Elena's Secrets of Mexican Cooking, Zelayeta, Elena *(Doubleday & Co.)*

Mexico: Her Daily & Festive Breads, Taylor, Barbara *(The Creative Press)*

Films

Basketry of the Pomo
U.C. 21 minutes. Color
Shows, through slow motion, some shapes and methods of making Pomo Indian baskets.

Basketry of the Pomo
U.C. 33 minutes.
The techniques of forming and decorating baskets is shown in some detail.

Basketry of the Pomo — Techniques
U.C. 30 minutes.
This film shows the California Pomo Indian women gathering and preparing the material, including feathers and beads, for their basket making. They are shown demonstrating somestechniques.

Candle Making
Barr. 11 minutes.
The dipping method of making candles is shown in some detail.

California
Oxford Films. 12 minutes.
An overview of California's history and geography are given. This is a good background builder.

California Dawn
Consolidated Films. 27 minutes. Color
California's history from Cabrillo's discovery to the signing of the constitution.

California's Geographical Regions
Barr. 11 minutes. Color
The six regions are shown, compared and contrasted: North coast, south coast, Sierra Nevadas and the Central Valley. This helps all who view it to understand better the topographical differences and similarities of California.

California — Geography, Weather, Water
Avis. 20 minutes.
A broad overview of geography, weather and water is shown as they interact.

California Missions
R.K.O. 10 minutes.
This film shows the Mission trail and traces the history and development of the Mission to show their purposes. The Missions are shown as they are today and portrayed as they were originally.

California Picture Book
United World. 9 minutes.
The Monterey Peninsula, Santa Barbara, Los Angeles, and the giant redwoods are showin in their dramatic glory.

The Dream That Became California
Cypress. 18 minutes. Color
This film gives a brief historical account of Spanish life in California, particularly of the Mission system.

Grapes
Barr. 11 minutes. Color
Grape growing is a principle agricultural product started by the Mission fathers. Shows growing, harvesting and shipping in California's vineyard country.

The Indians of California, Parts I and II
Barr. 29 minutes.
Trading, cradle and basket making, house building, deer hunting, gathering and preparing acorns are among the aspects of California Indian life shown.

Mission Life
Barr. 22 minutes.
The daily activities of the Mission Indians are pictured as they were at their height. The narration is by a padre writing in his journal.

Mission of California
B.F.A. 22 minutes.
The contributions and influences of the Missions on early California life is depicted.

Missions, Ranchos and Americans
Oxford Films. 14 minutes. Color
California's roots are shown through such sources as a diary and the period folk art. The heart of the film is the Spanish beginnings of California.

The Orange Grower
16 minutes. Color
Film shows the development of orange growing in California from Mission groups to the big business it has become.

Spinning Wheel
Barr. 10 minutes. Color
Wood carding, rolling, and spinning are shown.

Weaving Looms You Can Make
A.C.I. 16 minutes.
Simple homemade looms are shown which might turn your children into a weaving group of Mission Indians.

Indian Life — Check with a school materials center for producer and availability of these films:

Concow
Film about the Concow Indians and includes much plant use information.

Acorns and Buckeyes
Effectively presents the food processing of leaching, etc.

Bryan Beavers
Film about an old timer and his particular life style.